Ransomware

Ransomware is a threat variant that has existed for a very long time, contrary to popular belief. Today, ransomware attacks have become much more covert and stealthier than when they first came out. In this book, the author provides an overview of ransomware and the timeline of its evolution.

The author also discusses famous ransomware attacks that have occurred, with a special focus on SolarWinds and critical infrastructure before taking a deep dive into penetration testing and how it can be used to mitigate the risks of a ransomware attack from happening. The author also covers incident response, disaster recovery, and business continuity planning. We even look at an appropriate data backup plan as well.

Ravindra Das is a technical writer in the cybersecurity realm. He does cybersecurity consulting on the side through his private practice, RaviDas.Tech, Inc. He also holds the Certified in Cybersecurity certification from the ISC2.

Cyber Shorts Series

Ransomware: Penetration Testing and Contingency Planning
Ravindra Das

Deploying the Zero Trust Framework in MSFT Azure
Ravindra Das

For more information about the series: www.routledge.com/Cyber-Shorts/book-series/CYBSH

Ransomware
Penetration Testing and Contingency Planning

Ravindra Das

CRC Press
Taylor & Francis Group
Boca Raton London New York

CRC Press is an imprint of the
Taylor & Francis Group, an **informa** business

Designed cover image: ©ShutterStock Images

First edition published 2024
by CRC Press
2385 NW Executive Center Drive, Suite 320, Boca Raton FL 33431

and by CRC Press
4 Park Square, Milton Park, Abingdon, Oxon, OX14 4RN

CRC Press is an imprint of Taylor & Francis Group, LLC

© 2024 Ravindra Das

ISBN: 978-1-032-55667-3 (hbk)
ISBN: 978-1-032-55669-7 (pbk)
ISBN: 978-1-003-43163-3 (ebk)

DOI: 10.1201/9781003431633

Typeset in Minion Pro
by Apex CoVantage, LLC

*This book is dedicated to my Lord and Savior, Jesus Christ, the
Grand Designer of the Universe, and to my parents,
Dr. Gopal Das and Mrs. Kunda Das.
This book is also dedicated to:
Richard and Gwynda Bowman
Jaya Chandra
My loving cats, Fifi and Bubu*

Contents

Acknowledgment

I WOULD LIKE TO THANK Ms. Gabrielle Williams, my editor, who made this book into a reality.

Introduction

W E ARE LIVING IN a world today that is more connected than ever before. Looking back at the 1980s, of course life was much simpler back then. Color TV and landline phones were the norm; nobody even gave a thought as to how the world would evolve today. That was the time of the Cold War, and the biggest fear back then was when the nuclear missiles would be launched and when they would reach their target.

But now of course, things are totally different. We are living in a world where everything is all connected. There are smartphones, social media sites (primarily those of Facebook, Twitter (now X), LinkedIn, Instagram, Pinterest, etc.), and apps that seem to be growing every day. Gone are the days when we had to physically meet with people to get our daily job tasks done and accomplished. With all the interconnectivity that is happening today, there is no longer the need to have these direct, face-to-face types and kinds of dialogues.

THE COVID-19 PANDEMIC

The primary driver for this, of course, has been COVID-19, the pandemic that turned the world upside down and in ways never even imagined. Although this was a horrific experience to have lived through and many sad things have happened because of it (such as the sheer amount of people dying), there was some good that actually came out of it.

For example, before COVID-19 even hit, it would take years for the Food and Drug Administration (FDA) to approve a new vaccination to

DOI: 10.1201/9781003431633-1

come onto the market. There would be hundreds of clinical trials, and the literally hundreds of pages (or even thousands) of data that a pharmaceutical company would have to present to the FDA. But with the pandemic, there was a dire need to create a vaccine so that people would no longer die.

Within an approximate six-month time frame, Pfizer came out with the first vaccine, and it was very quickly approved by the FDA. Following suit was the Moderna vaccine, then the Johnson & Johnson vaccine. Eventually, there were more many pharmaceutical companies coming out with their own kinds of COVID-19 vaccines, in an effort to break up the monopolies that were held by both Pfizer and Moderna.

Even China came out with its version of the vaccine, which was called "Sinovax". So, as one can see, the good news here is that it does not take as long of a time now to get a vaccine to market. So, if there were to be another pandemic, the chances are now much greater that a vaccine will be formulated and approved very quickly. The second good thing to come out of the COVID-19 pandemic was the remote workforce.

Now, the concept of having employees working remotely is nothing new. It has been around for quite a long time, and technically, it was known as "telecommuting". But what was not imagined or even perceived was the degree to which the so-called remote workforce would take hold. For example, the notion of a 99% remote workforce was imagined to take place in four or five years from now.

But because of the COVID-19 pandemic, this all happened in a matter of literally three months. Employees were told to work from home, with no clear sight as to when they could return to an office-based environment. One of the benefits of this is that it gave employees a chance for a more flexible work schedule and to structure their daily job tasks the way they wanted to. But of course, there were downsides of this as well. Probably the biggest one of these relates to cybersecurity. For example, companies were in a huge rush to get employees to work from home (WFH) and because of that, they were hastily scrambling company-issued devices. With this haste, not all the proper security protocols were put into place, and because of that, many cybersecurity issues evolved quickly.

The Cyber Threats that Have Evolved from COVID-19

Probably the first one was the meshing of the home networks of the employees with that of the corporate networks. This led to the creation of many backdoors, and the IT Security Teams had no way of patching or even remediating them because of the personal nature of the employees' networks. As a result, the cyberattackers could not only penetrate the employee's home network, but from there, they could even penetrate the corporate network as well.

Second, if the remote employee was not given a company-issued device, they would then often rely upon their own devices to conduct their daily job tasks, primarily which would be the smartphone. But most of the time, these personal devices did not have the cyber standards built into them as was mandated by the company security policy. So, if the remote employee lost their smartphone, or if it was stolen, then the confidential and private information of the company that was on the device would also be at grave risk.

Zoombombing

Third, since everybody for the most part was working remotely and there was no direct face-to-face contact, having meetings and other forms of communications thus took place on video conferencing. At the time, Zoom was the biggest vendor, and because of that, it bore the brunt of the cyberattacker. For example, the most common threat to this platform was what is known as "Zoombombing". A technical definition of it is as follows:

> Zoombombing is a type of cyber-harassment in which an individual or a group of unwanted and uninvited users interrupt online meetings over the Zoom video conference app. This disruption occurs when intruders gate-crash gatherings – sometimes for malicious purposes, such as sharing pornographic or hate images or shouting offensive language – without the host's permission.
>
> (SOURCE: www.techtarget.com/searchsecurity/
> definition/Zoombombing)

In simpler terms, this is when a group of people or coworkers would be having a meeting, and all of a sudden, an unknown and uninvited guest would simply appear and produce unwanted interruptions. Over time, Zoom came out with various patches and software upgrades that would help to remediate this huge problem. However, Microsoft Teams came out into the limelight and was favored as a huge alternative to Zoom.

The Virtual Private Network

Fourth, another major cyber issue that also evolved over time was that of the virtual private network, also known as the "VPN" for short. This is a technology that was (and still continues to be) a way to provide a secure means for the remote worker to log into the corporate networks in order to gain access to the shared resources, which were needed for them to conduct their daily job tasks. A technical definition of a VPN is as follows:

> A virtual private network, or VPN, is an encrypted connection over the Internet from a device to a network. The encrypted connection helps ensure that sensitive data is safely transmitted. It prevents unauthorized people from eavesdropping on the traffic and allows the user to conduct work remotely. VPN technology is widely used in corporate environments.
>
> (SOURCE: www.cisco.com/c/en/us/products/security/
> vpn-endpoint-security-clients/what-is-vpn.html)

An example of a VPN is illustrated next:

Typically, a VPN works very well when used by a remote workforce that is only populated by 20%–30% of workers. But the technology took its maximum when the nearly 99% remote workforce suddenly came by storm. It took a huge toll on it, and because of that, it literally broke under this strain, leaving many holes open now for the cyberattacker. So, what was once a tried and tested security tool now became vulnerable.

In response to this, just like to the Zoombombing threat, the larger cyber companies came out with a new tool called the "Next Generation Firewall" to remediate the new weaknesses that became apparent with the VPN. This is examined more closely in the next subsection.

The Next Generation Firewall – The Substitute for the VPN
The Inherent Weaknesses of the Firewall (VPN)

There are key security issues that are inherent with the traditional firewall, which are as follows:

1) *Slow network performance*:

While the firewall has been primarily designed to allow for an end user to log in securely from just about any remote connection, the gravity of the number of people trying to use this mechanism all at once has greatly slowed down the flow of network communications from the point of origination to the point of destination, and vice versa. For example, most firewalls have been designed and implemented in such a way that it can only handle about 20%–30% of the workforce working remotely, not 100% of them. Also, because the firewall have been so widely trusted before the advent of the pandemic, many businesses across corporate America have also disregarded the importance of setting up baseline metrics to determine if their firewall infrastructure is indeed working up to optimal standards in today's environment. Because of the surge of remote employees on a global basis, there is an increased trend with the total number of dropped connections that are taking place. When this happens, there is usually a "kill-switch" feature, in which the firewall connection is automatically disconnected. When this happens and the remote employee is unaware of it, he or she is no longer online anonymously. Their IP address is immediately exposed to the public Internet.

2) *Companies may not be using enterprise grade firewall software:*

Many businesses, especially the small to medium-sized businesses (SMBs), may not even have been using any sort of firewall before the pandemic hit. But in a rush to secure these connections as their employees started to work from home, many business owners probably purchased a rather cheap firewall software package from an Internet service provider (ISP). At this point, keep in mind that the connection from the firewall to the corporate servers is not one straight, linear shot. Rather, there are many nodes in between in which the connections may traverse through before they reach their final destination. Some of these nodes could even exist in other countries where the data and privacy laws are not so stringent as they are here in the United States. As a result, depending upon where the ISP is using these specific nodes, the firewall package that has been purchased could very well be prone to data leakage and interception from malicious third parties during the time the network connection was established and being used until the remote employee has logged off from his or her session.

3) *The intermingling with the home network:*

With the remote work environment becoming a permanent reality now because of COVID-19, many home-based routers are now being used to actually connect to the firewall interface. While the home network may be secure to some degree or another, this kind of connection brings along with it its own set of security vulnerabilities. For example, if there are any malicious payloads that have been unknowingly downloaded, these can also reach the servers of the business as well, as the flow of network communications is being transmitted back and forth. Even worse, this kind of connection can even become permanent in nature, which is technically known as a site-to-site firewall. In other words, whatever kinds of digital goods you have downloaded onto your home network will also have an equal, if not greater access to the network infrastructure of the business. This will only further enhance the risk level of the personal identifiable information (PII) records of customers to possible third-party interception. Also, many remote employees are using their own personal computers or wireless devices to conduct their everyday job functions. As a result, there could be compatibility issues with the firewall that is being used, thus increasing the attack surface even more.

The Next Generation Firewall

Many cybersecurity professionals agree that the age of the traditional firewall could be seeing its last days in just a matter of a rather short time period, since the trend of WFH now seems to be an exceptionally long-term one. Because of this, other solutions are currently being examined, especially that of the Next Generation Firewall. Here are some of the key advantages that it brings to the table:

1) *It achieves full network traffic visibility:*

   As mentioned earlier, with the co-mingling of both the home network and the business firewall, it has become much more difficult for the network administrator to actually pinpoint and diagnose any network glitches, bottlenecks, or hiccups. But with the Next Gen Firewall, this should not be an issue. The primary reason for this is that it inspects each and every data packet that is being transmitted, whether they are at the various Internet Gateways, in the external or internal environments, or even on a cloud-based platform such as that of the Microsoft Azure or the AWS.

2) *Threat vectors are stopped immediately:*

   By using advanced techniques like those of artificial intelligence (AI), the Next Gen Firewall can stop just about any kind of cyberattack from happening before they become a true menace. For example, this includes previously known and newer threat vectors, as well as those types of highly specialized malware that can evade detection by antispyware and antimalware software packages that have been deployed at the endpoints. For those remote workers who are using their mobile devices to conduct their daily job functions, all network traffic is very carefully scrutinized by an automated threat detection agent.

3) *Access to SaaS-based applications is tightly controlled:*

   For those businesses that have deployed their entire IT infrastructure to the cloud, the remote employees will be primarily accessing applications that are SaaS-based. The Next Gen Firewall carefully monitors all access activity that is taking place, so that no rogue applications can be deployed that could cause further damage.

4) *The Zero Trust Framework is automatically implemented*:

With the traditional firewall, there is a certain level of trust with remote employees that is maintained. This is dependent of course on job titles/functions, as well as the rights and permissions that have been granted to every individual. But the Next Gen Firewall has no level of trust like this, in that it requires all the remote employees to go through the same layers of authentication, if not more.

5) *It creates secure access points to external third parties*:

It could be the case that a business has implemented the use of a fire-wall structure, but their outside suppliers or other third parties that they have outsourced certain business functions have not. Of course, this is a grave security vulnerability, as it leaves the network lines of communications open to the entire public Internet. The Next Gen Firewall does away with this weakness altogether, by implement-ing the use of a clientless SSL protocol in which all connections are made invisible to the external environment through a sophisticated web-based client.

Strategic Benefits	Next Gen Firewall	Traditional Firewall (VPN)
Provides for remote access	Yes	Yes
Secure connectivity is ensured to some degree or another	Yes	Yes
Protects against threat vectors posed to cloud-based platforms and SaaS applications	Yes	No
Mitigates against the risk of identity theft	Yes	No
Fortifies internal networks	Yes	No
Deploys the Zero Trust Framework	Yes	No
Implements access rules and policies that permit for high levels of visibility and granular control, based upon the following characteristics:	Yes	No

- The remote employee;
- Type of device;
- Content and/or applications being accessed.

So as one can see, another key advantage gained from the COVID-19 pandemic was that of newer technology evolving to further enhance or even totally replace existing ones, like the VPN. An example of a Next Generation Firewall is illustrated next:

Ransomware

Fifth, the next major cyber threat that quickly evolved as a result of the COVID-19 pandemic was ransomware. For the most part, we all have heard of ransomware. This is where a cyberattacker deploys a piece of malicious payload into your device. This can come from a phishing attack, such as clicking on a malicious link or downloading an infected attachment, such as a Word document, a PowerPoint presentation, or even an Excel file.

Once this malicious payload makes its way into your system, it then literally locks it up and holds your device hostage. Further, it will even encrypt your files. Theoretically, the only way out of this is to pay the cyberattacker a rather hefty ransom, usually paid by a virtual currency, such as that of a Bitcoin, or something similar. Once this is paid, the cyberattacker, if they are "ethical" enough will then send you the algorithm to decrypt your files and restore your wireless device back to normal.

Although this is how ransomware attacks have typically occurred, they have become much more sinister in nature. For example, they now have become extortion-like attacks (this is where the cyberattacker threatens to make public all the personal identifiable information (PII) datasets he or she has stolen), or even sell them on the Dark Web (this will be discussed later in the book).

But apart from all of this, during the COVID-19 pandemic, ransomware also evolved to become the creation of phony and fictitious websites. This is where a cyberattacker would either directly heist a particular domain or come up with something very similar. For example, rather than trying to directly steal Walmart.com, the cyberattacker could register a very similar domain like wal-mart.com. From here, a phony but very realistic website would then be created to lure unsuspecting victims. This kind of cyberattack is also known as "typo-squatting". A technical definition of it is as follows:

> Typosquatting is what we call it when people – often criminals – register a common misspelling of another organization's domain as their own. For example: tailspintoy.com instead of tailspintoys. com (note the missing "s").
>
> If you mistype or misspell the legitimate site you'll get the typo-squatter's site instead and it may not always be obvious that you're not where you intended to go.
>
> (SOURCE: https://support.microsoft.com/en-gb/topic/what-is-typosquatting-54a18872-8459-4d47-b3e3-d84d9a362eb0).

This is also known as "URL hijacking". Ransomware is still very prevalent today and will continue to be so for a very long time to come. It will continue to get much more advanced and much more sophisticated in nature. A technical definition of ransomware is as follows:

> Ransomware is a type of malware (malicious software) that locks a victim's data or device and threatens to keep it locked – or worse – unless the victim pays a ransom to the attacker. According to the IBM Security X-Force Threat Intelligence Index 2023, ransomware attacks represented 17 percent of all cyberattacks in 2022.
>
> (SOURCE: www.ibm.com/topics/ransomware)

The earliest ransomware attacks simply demanded a ransom in exchange for the encryption key needed to regain access to the affected data or use of the infected device. By making regular or continuous data backups, an organization could limit costs from these types of ransomware attacks and often avoid paying the ransom demand.

> But in recent years, ransomware attacks have evolved to include double-extortion and triple-extortion attacks that raise the stakes considerably – even for victims who rigorously [maintain] data backups or pay the initial ransom demand. Double-extortion attacks add the threat of stealing the victim's data and leaking it online; on top of that, triple-extortion attacks threaten to use the stolen data to attack the victim's customers or business partners.

(SOURCE: www.ibm.com/topics/ransomware)

An example of ransomware is illustrated next:

OVERVIEW OF THE BOOK

In this book, we will be doing a deeper dive into ransomware and one of the best ways to remediate, which is pen testing. A breakdown of this book is as follows:

Chapter 1: An overview of ransomware

Chapter 2: The anatomy of a ransomware attack and famous examples

Chapter 3: Penetration testing, one of the best tools for ransomware remediation

Chapter 4: How to recover from a ransomware attack: incident response, disaster recovery, and business continuity

The History of Ransomware

B ELIEVE IT OR NOT, ransomware is really not anything new. It goes back a long time, well even before phishing became a household term. The only reason we hear so much about it now in the news headlines is that there have been many more attacks that involved ransomware as of late. As it will be explored in more detail, the greatest fear of a ransomware attack is not so much the digital types of attacks that have been so prevalent, but rather, the real damage will come when there is a large-scale ransomware attack that is launched onto our critical infrastructure systems. In this section, we review the chronological timetable of how ransomware actually evolved, and how it has become the large-scale threat today.

The Year 1989

The World Health Organization (WHO) held its conference about the disease known as the acquired immune deficiency syndrome (AIDS). The organizer of this 1989 conference, a professor of biology from Harvard University by the name of Joseph L. Popp actually mailed out 20,000 floppy disks to all the conference attendees. An example of this kind of disk is illustrated next:

Supposedly, the floppy disk in question appeared to have a questionnaire in it, which would give the recipient the ability to assess if somebody they know has AIDS. But in reality, this floppy disk contained a malicious

DOI: 10.1201/9781003431633-2

payload, and because of that, all 20,000 (and perhaps even more) were infected by it. Soon enough, this became the first true ransomware attack, and it was called the "AIDS Trojan".

From here, all the files on the victim's computers were encrypted, and a ransom of $189.00 was demanded. Of course, virtual currencies like Bitcoin did not exist at the time, so a check was demanded to be sent to an unknown address in Panama. But the good news here is that since this malicious payload was actually quite easy to reverse engineer, IT Security specialists at the time were able to come up rather quickly with a decryption algorithm, so that the victims could gain control of their computers once again. Because of this, Joseph L. Popp became known affectionately as the "Father of Ransomware".

The Internet Explosion

After this first incidence, there were no known ransomware attacks for at least the next 15 years. But as the dot com craze exploded into the late 1990s and shifted over into 2000, ransomware started to gain notoriety yet once again. Two powerful variants (as deemed at the time) came out that were known as:

- GPCode

- Archievus

The GPCode sent to victims malicious links and even phishing-based E-mails. Keep in mind that phishing also evolved publicly for the first time in the late 90s as well, when America Online (AOL) was infected by it. Again, it locked up files, and the cyberattackers at the time only demanded $20 as the ransom payment. But just like the AIDS Trojan, the encryption algorithm was easily cracked, so in the end, the victims could gain control of their devices rather quickly.

But the Archievus malicious payload was a much more powerful strain. The creators of this variant understood that a strong encryption algorithm would be needed to launch a successful ransomware attack. As a result, they chose to use the RSA algorithm, which at the time, had a 1,024 bit encryption key. However, where the cyberattackers failed in this instance is that they did not create strong passwords, and because of this once again, the victims of this ransomware attack were able to recover pretty quickly.

So, as you can see, during this time the focus was primarily on the total number of ransomware attacks that could be launched and not their sophistication.

The 2010 Decade

In this decade, the ransomware strains became much more powerful than ever before. For example, the "Locker" variant emerged, and the virtual currencies started to make their appearance in the financial markets. During this time frame, three powerful variants emerged, which are as follows:

1) *The Winlock*:

   As just mentioned, this was the first true "Locker" type of ransomware variant. In fact, this was the first deemed to truly lock the victims out of their devices.

2) *The Reveton*:

   This variant first came out in 2012. This was the first one to use what is known as "Ransomware as a Service", also known as "RaaS" for short. Just like you have probably heard of the IaaS, SaaS, and PaaS (all which stand for Infrastructure as a Service, Software as a Service, and Platform as a Service, respectively), the RaaS is an actual service that a cyberattacker can rent out to hire a third party to actually launch the attacks. This was available all on the Dark Web (which will be examined in more detail in Chapter 2 of this book), and the message that was used by the cyberattacker in this instance accused the victims of a crime that they never committed. And, if they did not pay up, they would be reported to law enforcement. It should also be noted here that this was the first ransomware attack that demanded the actual ransom via a virtual currency, namely Bitcoin.

3) *The CryptoLocker*:

This was the first ransomware strain that used a more powerful version of the RSA algorithm. This time, it was a 2,048 bit encryption key, but what was unique about this one is that it was Locker and a Crypto variant. It was primarily used in phishing attacks, but the malicious payloads were deployed from attachments that were downloaded onto the victim's computer. During this time frame, this was the most "profitable" ransomware attack. The cyberattackers were able to gain ransom payments of close to $27 million in just two months.

During 2015

Up until this point in time, all the ransomware variants just reviewed had only one primary target: the Windows-based devices. Pretty much all the operating systems that Microsoft came out with became a target. The cyberattackers have not yet targeted another popular operating system, which was Linux – that is, until 2015. Two new ransomware variants were specifically created for this task, and they are as follows:

1) *The Simple Locker*:

This was the first ransomware strain that was used to encrypt and lock up files that were native to the Android operating system. This targeted secure digital cards, also known as "SD Cards". An example of this is illustrated next:

This variant targeted all kinds of files for the first time, which included documents, images, and even videos.

2) *The Locker Pin*:

This ransomware strain also directly targeted Android operating systems. But what was different about this one was that it did not just encrypt files from within the wireless device, but it also locked out the victims from even trying to access them as well. Also, the PIN number of the victim was covertly changed. A newer version of this variant eventually came out, and this was known as the "Linux. Encoder.1". It was specifically created and designed for targeting the Linux operating system.

2016–2020

In 2016, a ransomware variant known as "Ransom 32" was the strain to impact JavaScript, which is a scripting language used heavily to create web-based applications. During this time frame, ransomware now emerged globally; four new variants were launched, which include the following:

1) *The Petya*:

This was the first ransomware strain to actually lock up the master boot record of a device and even its master file table. This was also the first time that a variant locked up the entire hard drive.

2) *The Zcryptor*:

This was the first ransomware variant to use Worms. Because of it, this strain became particularly deadly, because it could literally replicate itself in just a matter of minutes. This became technically known as a "Ransomworm".

3) *The WannaCry*:

This has been deemed to be one of the deadliest ransomware variants ever to be launched. It infected in a short time period over 100,000 devices across 150 countries. All kinds of industries and businesses were impacted, ranging from law enforcement to healthcare. This strain also spread and distributed a vulnerability known as "Eternal Blue".

4) *The Golden Eye*:

This ransomware variant is a combination of the Petya and WannaCry strains, by having even more powerful encryption algorithms deployed into it.

5) *The NotPetya*:

This ransomware strain variant not only locked up files, but it could also delete them, if the victim did not pay up the ransom in a timely manner.

The 2020s

This decade has seen the evolution of not only new kinds of ransomware strains but also the end goals the cyberattacker has in mind. Two new trends have evolved, and they are as follows:

1) *Double Extortion*:

As it was touched earlier in this chapter, not only is the cyberattacker of today taking over entire devices and systems, but now they are threatening extortion if payment is not made. This can include releasing any private or confidential information to the public or selling them on the Dark Web for a rather nice profit.

2) *Big Game Hunting*:

This is where the cyberattacker primarily targets the larger corporations and businesses, based solely on the premises that they can pay up more. The selection of targets is based upon a certain set of criteria. Usually, cyberattackers of today spend several months covertly stalking the IT system of a business before installing malware. The length of time big hunters is in your system is frightening. The common exploits here are the weaknesses found in the remote desktop protocol (RDP) and servers. Some examples of high-profile targets include the cities of Baltimore and Atlanta (in the United States), the Colonial Pipeline, and JBS Foods.

In 2021, one of the largest ransomware attacks occurred, and the strain was known as the "REvil Raas". More than one million devices were affected, and the cyberattackers demanded a total of $70 million to be made in ransom payments.

This entire history of ransomware is illustrated in the following diagram:

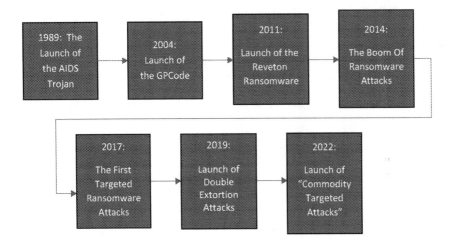

The Differences between Malware and Ransomware

Throughout this chapter so far, we have used the terms "malware" and "ransomware" interchangeably. Although the two have similarities, they have distinct differences as well, and it is important to point them out, in the following matrix:

Malware	Ransomware
It is a piece of malicious code, which can cause all sorts of damages to any kind or type of device.	Designed specifically to lock up a device so it is rendered useless until ransom is paid.
Can be delivered by numerous mechanisms.	Primarily uses phishing.
Malicious code can be removed with the appropriate antivirus or antimalware software package.	It is very difficult, if not impossible to remove.
It can cause severe degradation to the device.	The device gets totally locked, and nobody except for the cyberattacker can access it.

In the next few sections, we examine other areas of ransomware on a broader, or macro basis.

HOW RANSOMWARE IS DEPLOYED

There are two primary ways in which your computer can get infected with ransomware, apart from what has been reviewed thus far in this chapter.

1) *Via MalSpam*:

This is essentially a spam e-mail that comes into your inbox, but it contains a malware-based. EXE code that will launch itself once the attachment is downloaded and opened. These types of attachments are typically. DOC,. PPT, and. XLS files. You can also get ransomware by clicking on a phony link in the content of the e-mail message. The techniques of social engineering are very often used in this regard to make the e-mail look like it is authentic and coming from either a trusted, legitimate organization or personal contact.

2) *Via Malvertising*:

This is when a cyberattacker uses online advertising to capture the unwitting attention of the end user and ensnare them into clicking on a genuine-looking hyperlink. If this does happen, then the servers that are used by the cyberattacker will collect details about the soon-to-be victim's computer, including its geographical location.

Once this has been accomplished, then the ransomware attack is subsequently launched. Malvertising very often uses what is known as an infected "iframe". This is an invisible webpage element and will redirect the end user to an authentic-looking landing page. From there, the malicious code is then deployed onto the end user's computer.

THE TYPES OF RANSOMWARE ATTACKS

There are three types of ransomware attacks:

1) *Scareware*:

As the name implies, this kind of attack is just merely designed to scare or frighten you. These kinds of attacks primarily use annoying pop messages. One of the most "famous" of these is the pop up, which claims that some sort of malware has been detected on your computer, and to get rid of it, you have to pay a small ransom. You will know if you have been hit by this kind of ransomware attack if these pop ups keep constantly appearing. The only way to get rid of them is to install antimalware software, such as the ones available from Norton and Kaspersky.

2) *Screen Lockers*:

This is the next step up in terms of the severity level of ransomware attacks. With this, your computer screen locks up, and as a result, you are completely frozen from accessing your files and folders. To make matters even worse, the message that appears will typically have an FBI, Secret Service, or a Department of Justice official seal, to make it look like that you have been caught doing some sort of illicit activity online. To unfreeze your screen, there will also be a message that you have pay a rather hefty fine. But keep in mind that these government agencies would never ask you to pay up. Probably the best way to get your screen unlocked is to take it to a local Geek Squad to clean your computer of the ransomware. If this doesn't work, you may then have to get a new computer altogether.

3) *Encrypting Ransomware*:

These are deemed to be the worst kind of attack. In these particular instances, the cyberattacker will steal your files and encrypt them with a very complex mathematical algorithm, which will be very difficult to crack. To get your files back, the cyberattacker will demand a large amount of money, to be paid by Bitcoin. Once they get this money, they claim that they will send to you the decryption key to not only retrieve your files, but to unscramble them as well into a decipherable state (in other words, making them like they were before they were hijacked). But most often this never happens, because once you pay up, the cyberattacker often disappears. Since you have paid with a virtual currency, there is no way of tracking them down either (unlike paper currency, where you can use marked bills for these purposes).

HOW THE CISO AND THEIR IT SECURITY TEAM CAN HELP MITIGATE AN EXTORTION-STYLE ATTACK

Ransomware extortion attacks have gotten so bad that it is expected to cost corporate America $265 billion by 2031.[1] So, what can a CISO do to help mitigate the risks of being hammered three times over by a cyberattacker? Here are some key tips:

1) *Know thy data*:

   Being the head of your IT Security Team, it is ultimately you, the chief information security officer (CISO), who must take responsibility for knowing what kinds of information and data are being collected and used by your company. But even more important is you need to know at all times where it is all being stored. Even to this day, a surprising number of CISOs still cannot provide an answer to this question when they are asked directly about it. If you really don't anything about it, then ask your IT Security Team to help you diagram where all of it is at.

2) *Get rid of the silos*:

   For the longest time, corporate America lived in what are called "silos". This simply means each department in a company merely did their own thing, without working as a team with the other teams. IT Security has been notorious for doing this, but now, with the advent of the 99% remote workforce, people are realizing that all departments have to come together at varying degrees for the common good of their employer. So, this approach should also work for your databases.

Rather than keeping ten different bases, it is probably even wiser to consolidate all of them into one central repository and from there move them into a cloud platform, such as Microsoft Azure. In fact, a lot of cyber pundits are now calling for this kind of centralization. Why is this? Well, your data becomes easier to manage and optimize, and you can implement all of them into one place. Thus, it is also easier to keep track of any malicious behavior.

3) *Keep analyzing*:

With the help of both AI and machine learning (ML) tools, you can quickly analyze the data that you have, and what is incoming and even what is outgoing. Of course, the goal here should be to look for unusual patterns in network traffic, but you and your IT Security Team also need to keep creating new baseline profiles as the needs dictate them. In other words, you should never rely upon a static baseline for a long time. Your profile is a dynamic one and thus should be updated based upon what you see in the external and internal environments of your company.

4) *Incorporate PAM*:

This is an acronym that stands for "privileged access management". This methodology should be used when managing privileged accounts, especially those in a hybrid cloud environment. Essentially, these accounts can be viewed as "superuser" accounts in which higher than normal rights, privileges, and permissions are assigned to certain employees in a company. You should never rely upon manual process here. Your IT Security Team has enough to worry about, and you don't want any of your privileged accounts to be hijacked. A good PAM-based solution will help you to automatically delete and/or decommission those that are not in use anymore, or simply deemed to be inactive.

5) *Work proactively after the attack*:

After the dust has settled, you will then want to discover entry points where the cyberattacker was able to penetrate through. A good forensics analysis should help to reveal this, but only a penetration test can tell you what really happened. Therefore, you should run one immediately after the attack and immediately fill any gaps with the remediative steps that have been provided to you. But even after this, you should be running a deep pen test scan at least once every quarter. This can be expensive, but now many companies are coming with pen testing solutions from which you can get a license for a certain amount of time. This will let you run as many scans as you want or need to.

TWO OVERVIEWS OF RANSOMWARE ATTACKS

Probably one of the most famous examples of a large-scale ransomware attack was the one on the Colonial Gas Pipeline. In this case, the hacking group used malware to halt the flow of natural gas in the eastern United States.

This wreaked quite a bit of havoc, as there were shortages across multiple states, and even the futures markets on natural gas became very unstable. Many people became fearful, and as a result, started to hoard as much natural gas as they could. To resolve this, the CEO of Colonial Gas made a ransom payment of $4.4 million.

In the spring of 2021, another high-profile attack happened to JBS Foods, one of the largest meat processors in the world. There was no panic of meat or related food products, but the company paid out $11 million in Bitcoin to the cyberattackers. This has been deemed to be the largest ransomware payment yet so far.

Ransomware hacks can also be called "supply chain attacks". This is where the cyberattacker can use one point to infiltrate thousands of victims. Kaseya was the best example of this. In this case, the cyberattacker sent out a malicious update through a vulnerability found in Kaseya's virtual system administrator. From this single point, millions of devices were locked up and held for ransom.

The hacking group demanded that a $70 million payment be made. But before this was paid, fortunately the FBI was able to break into the servers of the hacking group and retrieve the decryption algorithms.

TO PAY OR NOT TO PAY???

A common question that gets asked these days is whether a ransom payment should be made. On one side of the coin, if payment is made, you should be able to gain access back on your hijacked device. Again, the reality of this happening is close to zero, but there are cases in which a cyberattacker has actually kept good on their promise and have delivered the decryption algorithm to the victim, once payment has been made.

But on the flip side of the coin, there is also the theory that once a payment is made, the cyberattacker knows now that they can keep targeting you over and over again, because they now know your vulnerabilities. Also, with each attack, the probability also increases that they will even ask for more money. The first thing that comes to mind is to make payment as quickly as possible. But before you do that (and it is recommended that you do not), there are some important considerations, which are as follows:

1) The cyberattacker or hacking group wants to be paid via virtual currency. The primary reason for this is that if a traditional currency is to be used, it can easily be tracked down. Therefore, to avoid this, you will have to make the payment via Bitcoin (as this is the preferred payment method). If you are not familiar with the virtual currency world, it can take quite some time for you to get this money rounded up.

2) Once you have made payment and sent it off to wherever it needs to go, there is no guarantee whatsoever that you will receive the unlocking mechanism for your computer and the files. The cyberattacker will likely simply disappear somewhere and prey on another unsuspecting victim. There have actually been a few hacking groups that have lived up to their pledge and have delivered the tools you need for unlocking. But this is a dicey situation to be in. If you pay and get your items in return, there is an excellent chance the cyberattacker will come back after you again because they now know where your vulnerabilities and weak spots are. Who knows, in this second round, they may even ask for more than your business can even afford.

3) Paying off the cyberattacker like this is now starting to become a crime. For example, the US federal government can charge you with treason if you make payment to any of the nations that are deemed state threat actors. Also, many insurance companies will not even pay out your claim if you do make a ransom payment. But exceptions have been made, especially if the attack involved critical infrastructure. An excellent example of this is the Colonial Gas Pipeline hack. In the end, the CEO agreed to pay the $4 million ransom just to keep the flow of natural gas moving. Had this not happened, it is quite likely that the flow of natural gas would have been abruptly halted, causing prices to spike even higher.

HOW NOT TO MAKE A RANSOMWARE PAYMENT

You may be asking next, what can you do to prevent from making a ransom payment? The truth of the matter is there is nothing you can do directly. We are all at risk from the aforementioned situation happening. *The key is how to actually lessen the odds or mitigate that risk from happening to you and your business.* Here are some essential tips to keep in mind:

- Always keep backups on a daily schedule. Thus, if you are hit, all you technically have to do is to replace the hardware that has been affected and restore those with the backups. In this manner, it is highly recommended that you keep one set on-site and the other off-site, just so that you have some level of redundancy at hand.

- Think about moving to an on-cloud infrastructure. With this, you will have all the tools you need to create backups automatically. The two providers that offer all you need in this regard are Microsoft Azure and AWS. What is advantageous here is that you will not be dealing with hardware directly. Instead, you will be creating what is known as virtual machines (aka VMs), which are the software emulations of the hardware. So, if any of these VMs are impacted by a security breach, you can quickly delete them and create brand new VMs in just a few minutes.

ANOTHER WAY FOR THE CYBERATTACKER TO LAUNCH A RANSOMWARE ATTACK

Apart from the ways reviewed so far in this chapter in which a cyberattacker can launch a ransomware attack, another vehicle in which they can do it is by heisting the privileged accounts of the IT Security Team. These are the super user accounts in which access is granted to the entire IT and network infrastructures. This area falls under the realm of identity and access management (IAM). Consider some of these statistics:

- 51% of businesses have been impacted by ransomware.

- The cost of it to American businesses will soon reach $20 billion.

- The ransom demand will reach $200,000. But the demand escalates when the target is a high profile one. For example, in the Colonial Gas Pipeline attack, the ransom paid out was $4.4 million, though a big chunk of this was recouped by law enforcement.

- So far, one of the biggest ransom demands was from the cyberattack group that launched the hack against Bouygues, a construction company based in France: almost $12 million as payment.

- The average downtime cost to businesses was $283,000, which was twice as much from the year before.

- Just don't think that simply paying the ransom is the only cost that your business will bear. There is also the cost of recovery, both in the short and long terms. The average cost for this is a staggering $1.45 million.

- A ransomware attack occurs once every 11 seconds.

- Small to medium-sized businesses (SMBs) are now becoming a prime target for ransomware attacks. For example, 55% of the SMBs with an employee size of <500 and <$50 million in revenue have been impacted.

- Although the cyberattacker takes their time to study their targets, once the threat vector is launched, it acts quickly. For example, once the malicious payload has been deployed, it can cause maximum damage in just four hours. However, the fastest time was just under 45 seconds.

- Apart from the monetary damages, there is also another harm to businesses – actually having to shut down after being impacted. Consider this:

  - 764 healthcare organizations had to temporarily cease operations because of ransomware attacks.

  - 1,233 universities also had to temporarily close down, thus affecting the studies and graduation timetables of hundreds of students.

- Mobile ransomware has increased at least by 250%.

- Every 40 seconds, companies are hit by a ransomware attack.

- About $2,000 is the requested Ransom payment, though this is expected to increase. Keep in mind that cyberattackers want to be paid via Bitcoin, and even after you make payment, there is no guarantee that you will receive the decryption keys to unlock your files and computer.

- There are almost five times new ransomware variants.

- 72% of companies that have been hit by a cyberattack lose access to their mission critical information and data for at least two days and even longer.

- 67% of businesses that have been impacted by a ransomware attack have at least permanently lost part of their data.

- One in five SMBs paid their ransom via Bitcoin but never received the decryption keys that were promised.

- Almost 75% of businesses do not have the appropriate security mechanisms put into place to help thwart a ransomware attack.
  (SOURCES: www.cloudwards.net/ransomware-statistics/)

THE INGREDIENTS OF A RANSOMWARE PLAN

In the last chapter, we will review the importance of and the major components of having an incident response plan, a disaster recovery plan, and a business continuity plan. All of these documents will come into crucial play if you have been impacted by a ransomware attack. But in the meantime, this section will go over the major components of what you need in a ransomware plan as well.

Creating the ransomware plan will depend largely upon what your own security requirements are, but the bottom line is that you need something in hand that will let you recover in the quickest time possible. So, the following are the components *that must be included, as a baseline:*

1) *Create the response team:*

You will want to include people from the various departments that you have in your company. But take careful thought of who should be included. Obviously, the hourly contractor may not be the best choice; pick those people who understand what ransomware is all about. These should include folks from the IT Security Team, legal, human resources, as well as finance and accounting. Once you have assembled this team, assign specific roles and assignments to each member so they will know exactly what to do in case of a security breach.

2) *What the first response should be:*

If you are hit with a ransomware attack, you need to create a quick strategy of what will be done first. It is important to keep in mind that ransomware consists of malware and the type that can spread itself within minutes. Therefore, your first plan of attack should have all employees of the company immediately disconnect all devices that are connected to the network, so that they do not become infected. This alert should be in all forms of communication, such as phone calls, texts, and E-mails. Once this has been done, the response team can work on isolating the malware that has penetrated and mitigating any more damage. In fact, you should rehearse this kind of activity regularly, to see how long it does take for this to happen, and try to shorten that.

3) *Determine how communications will take place*:

This is perhaps one of the most crucial pieces of your ransomware plan. You need to create a call tree that will provide the direction on how the communications process will take place in case you are hit (in a way, this will be like a flowchart). Information to be put here includes the following:

- Phone numbers: this includes landlines and cell numbers;

- E-mail addresses: this includes both work and personal E-mails.

It is important to keep this information updated at all times. The people on your response team who are tasked with alerting the company will be primarily responsible for sending out the first round of messages to all employees. Initially, there could be some doubt if this is all real or not, so put out the same messaging on your company intranet as well. **Do not post anything on social media**, as this could be a temptation for other cyberattackers to launch other threat variants while you are dealing with the first attack.

4) *Have a data backup plan*:

Traditionally, this falls under the realm of the IT Security Team to create the backups and to execute them when needed, and the details of this should be included in your overall Security Plan. So far, the ransomware plan should contain the contact information of the people who will be doing this task. In fact, right after the first wave communications have gone would be the most optimal time to do this, so that they can get ready with the backups in place.

5) *Notify other key stakeholders*:

Once you have mitigated the ransomware breach to the best degree possible, it is important that you quickly notify other stakeholders as well. This will include the following groups of people:

- Shareholders;

- External, third-party vendors that you are currently working with;

- Law enforcement at all levels (this includes federal, state, and local agencies);

- The appropriate regulatory bodies.

It is important that you do this and not simply just ignore it. New laws have come out that now make it a felony for not reporting ransomware breaches in a timely fashion.

6) *Include information about your insurance policy*:

While you do not need to include every detail of your cybersecurity insurance policy, you should include the key tenets and provisions of it in ransomware plan, as a point of reference. Also, it is equally important to include the contact information of the people at the insurance company with whom will you be filing the claim. Of course, getting the ultimate payout is going to take some time; the sooner you get this ball rolling, the better off your company will be.

HOW TO MITIGATE THE RISKS OF RANSOMWARE ATTACK BY IMPLEMENTING PROPER IDENTITY AND ACCESS MANAGEMENT CONTROLS

The use of identity and access management (IAM) is a very strong and viable solution to help thwart any ransomware attacks. Essentially, IAM deals with three key areas, which involves the identification, authentication, and authorization of an individual who wants to gain access to certain resources. The major components that constitute an IAM solution include the following:

- An automated system of sorts that keeps a detailed log history of the login attempts and resource access by all the employees in your organization;

- The required tools for the creation, deletion, and revising of the rights, permissions, and privileges that are granted to all your employees;

- A comprehensive database (or even databases) that store all the login credentials and permissions granted to each employee.

Follow these guidelines when establishing your IAM Framework, especially when it comes to dealing with ransomware:

1) *Use role-based access controls*:

This is also referred to as "RBAC". With this, you need to carefully review each employee's job title and what their specific functions are. Once all of this has been ascertained, assign the permissions that are needed, at the bare minimum. This is also known as "least privilege access". In other words, you do not want to give an employee any more permission than what is absolutely required so they can perform job tasks daily. For example, you would not want to assign the employees of the finance department any sort of administrative privileges, which is far more appropriate for the network administrator.

2) *Use MFA*:

This is an acronym that stands for "multifactor authentication". With this, you are deploying at least three or more unique authentication methods to confirm the identity of an individual wanting to gain access to your IT and network infrastructure. This includes a combination of a password, a PIN number, an RSA token, and even a biometric-based technology such as that of fingerprint and/or iris recognition.

3) *Break out your network*:

Most businesses today still rely upon what is known as "perimeter security". This is where one large circle of defense is used to protect your digital assets. The main disadvantage with this methodology is that once the cyberattacker has broken through this, they can run free and gain access to just about anything they want to. In fact, this is how some of the ransomware attacks typically occur. To avoid this kind of scenario, seriously consider breaking up your IT and network infrastructure into various segments, which are also referred to as "Subnets". Each of one of these should have their own level of

MFA tools put into place. By taking this kind approach, the statistical chances of the cyberattacker breaking all the way through to the heart of your digital assets becomes almost zero.

MORE ABOUT THE RANSOMWARE GROUPS THEMSELVES

The common theme in this chapter has been examining the kind and types of ransomware threat variants that exist and some of the major attacks that have happened thus far. But what are the traits of the cyberattackers themselves?

1) *A definite classification scheme*:

Believe it or not, ransomware groups fall into certain categories, which are as follows:

- The Full Timers: these are the hacking groups that have been in existence for at least nine to ten months and have impacted at least ten or more victims. A good example of this is the LockBit group, which has accounted for at least 33% of ransomware attacks on a global basis. These kinds of groups have the money to have a good infrastructure, and most important (to them) is evading detection by law enforcement.

- The Rebrand Groups: these are the hacking groups that have been in business for less than nine months or so but are still just as active as the Full Timers. The only difference here is that they infiltrate more victims but stay in for a much shorter period of time. And their pace is rapid fire. They hit one victim, then move on to the next.

- The Splinter Groups: these are the cyberattackers that have broken off from one of the previous groups, as mentioned. Either they have decided to go solo or have joined another group with more "exciting opportunities". These kinds of cyberattackers are less known and are very erratic in their behaviors. In other words, they are trying to discover their own brand and identity.

- The Ephemeral Group: these are the groups that have been around for less than two months and launch a ransomware attack every now and then, with no defined frequency to it.

2) *A lot of rebranding*:

To evade law enforcement, like the FBI, most cyberattackers are constantly trying to go from one ransomware group to another. But this, of course, makes it harder for the IT Security team to keep track of, so the report claims that the sharing of intelligence with other entities (whether private or public) becomes very critical.

3) *It is getting far more difficult to negotiate*:

When ransomware attacks were just starting to happen, negotiating the payment was fairly straightforward, as the negotiator was just dealing with the same group. But with the advent of RaaS groups, negotiating has become very difficult, as there are now many more threat actors that are involved.

4) *The demands for payments are higher*:

In the early days of ransomware attacks, the costs of payments were rather low comparatively speaking, in the range of a few thousand to maybe perhaps a value in the five figures. But given the sophistication of the ransomware groups of today, the demands for large payments are now getting astronomical. For example, seeing something as high as $15 million is now not unheard of. But many ransomware negotiators are pretty successful at bringing this amount down, say something like in the six figures.

5) *Extortion is on the rise*:

Locking up your device and encrypting your files is one thing, but now ransomware groups are kicking up their degree of punishment by extorting their victims, as mentioned before. For instance, they can now exfiltrate your PII datasets and sell them on the Dark Web for a nice profit, or even threaten the victim to make them available to the public, thus causing brand and reputation damage, which is almost difficult to recover from. Why do they do this? Well, they figure if they are not going to get any money from the actual attack, perhaps threatening the victim on a much higher and personable level will result in getting some sort of payment.

THE OTHER TARGETS OF RANSOMWARE ATTACKS

This is one of the questions about ransomware that gets asked most next. The bottom line is that just about anybody or any business can become a victim. Even the targeted device can vary. It can be your hard-wired computer, your smartphone, or other form of wireless device.

There are no favored or heavily sought-after targets in this regard. In fact, if you have multiple devices, they could all be hit simultaneously, or even individually, at various intervals.

But there are favored industries that the cyberattacker likes to go after, and these include the following:

1) *Our own federal government*:

The US federal government is infamously known for using extremely outdated technology. Many of them still use unsupported software products, such as Windows 7 and 8. Also, there are some that still rely upon using mainframe-based components, such as the IRS. Because of this, deploying and applying the latest software patches and upgrades has become an impossible task. Worst yet, you simply cannot rip out these legacy systems and install new ones, as there will then be interoperability issues. Because of this, one of the prime directives of the Biden Executive Order on Improving the Nation's Cybersecurity is that the government, over a period of time, must start to replace these aging systems. Also, many of the agencies from within the federal government have not deployed any sort of endpoint protection, thus making them also a highly favored target in which malicious payloads are deployed upon.

2) *The Healthcare Industry*:

This is one of the very few market sectors in which controls and keeping devices up to date is actually happening, and the driving force behind this is HIPAA. But even despite this, ransomware has still impacted this industry hard. One of the reasons for this is that there is a lot more at stake to be captured other than just credit card numbers and passwords. There is the patient's medical history and related data. If this is hijacked, it is quite possible that the cyberattacker could even get access to the patient's medical device and launch covert attacks onto that. The effects of this can be devastating, such as possible loss of life of the individual if their particular device has been remotely tampered with.

3) *Colleges and universities*:

Before cyberattacks became the norm in our society today, many of the higher-level educational institutions felt that they would never become a prime target. As a result, there was very little effort to ramp up the level of security onto the campus servers and the workstations at the various computer labs. Because of this, segment also has become a favored target for ransomware attacks. One of the reasons for this is that younger students tend to be much more impressionable, and because of that, it is quite easy for them to fall victim to just about any type of threat variant. For example, phishing E-mails are used quite often, luring students into getting low interest loans, or even getting expensive textbooks for free. Also, a newer technique that has evolved is cyberattackers who are claiming to be freelancers with the promise of writing term papers for literally pennies on the dollar.

4) *The recruiting industry*:

Out of all the other segments reviewed in this chapter, this is probably the easiest one in which a cyberattacker can launch a ransomware campaign. One of the main reasons for that, even for a trained eye, is that it is very difficult to distinguish between what is real and fake. For example, with the COVID-19 pandemic, many phony and fictitious recruiting websites have been launched, using heisted domain names, which make them look like the real thing. Also, the use of social engineering tactics is used quite heavily here, with robocalls being placed mimicking genuine recruiters. Another technique used now more commonly is that of "smishing". This is when fake illegitimate text messages are sent to mobile devices with a link to click on. And if this happens, that particular wireless device will more than likely be used in a ransomware attack.

HOW TO AVOID THE RISKS OF BECOMING A VICTIM OF A RANSOMWARE ATTACK

It is important to keep in mind that everybody is prone to becoming a victim, whether it is an individual or a business. ***The key is in how to mitigate that risk of happening to you***. Here are some tips to follow:

1) *Use a cloud platform*:

With the remote workforce now taking a permanent hold, many organizations are now opting to move their on prem infrastructure entirely into the cloud now, using a well-known platform such as the AWS or Microsoft Azure. Although the cyberattacker is starting to target this area more now, the advantage of using the cloud is that you are already provided with a powerful set of security tools that you can deploy immediately to protect your digital assets. Most of these are included in your plan or just have a minimal cost if it is not. For instance, you can create dashboards to monitor your private cloud on a real-time basis, and many of the protective measures that are offered are often triggered automatically, depending upon the rules and conditions that you establish.

2) *Always conduct assessments*:

Whether your infrastructure is in the cloud or on prem, or even in both, it is always very important to conduct tests in order to find out where the unknown gaps and vulnerabilities are. One of the best ways to do this is via a penetration test. In this instance, it's probably best to outsource this particular function to a reputable, third-party vendor that specializes in doing this. That way, you will get a totally professional and unbiased assessment with recommendations on how to fill in the holes.

3) *Always make sure your team is ready*:

Keep in mind that apart from your security policy, the three other documents that are the most important to your business are as follows:

- Your incident response plan (which outlines how you will respond to a ransomware attack);

- Your disaster recovery plan (which spells out how you plan to get your most critical operations up and running in case you have been impacted);

- Your business continuity plan (which specifies how your business will recover in the long term from a ransomware attack).

Of these three, the first two are the most crucial. Therefore, it is imperative that you and your IT Security Team practice these drills regularly, so that all action items can happen seamlessly in a real-world situation. The last thing you need is your team guessing what needs to be done to fend off the ransomware attack. Equally important is to update these documents on a real-time basis with the lessons learned after you conduct each drill.

4) *Mandate the use of the Zero Trust Framework*:

With this methodology, you don't trust anybody whatsoever in both your internal and external environments, even those employees that have been with you the longest. True, it may sound extreme, but this is about one of the best ways right now to mitigate the risks of being hit. Under this approach, you break away from the notion of just one line of defense, and instead, have multiple ones of them. Each of these layers will have its own set of authentication mechanisms, which will be at least three or more. The idea here is that if a cyberattacker were to break through the first line of defense, the chances of them breaking through the others is greatly diminished.

5) *Always have backups*:

This has always been one of the cardinal rules in cybersecurity, but now it has taken on even more importance than ever before. For example, if you are impacted with a ransomware attack, you can essentially restore business operations almost immediately through the backups that you have created. But the key here is that creating backups is not just a one-time deal. Rather, it must be done regularly, preferably even doing it at least two times to three times a day. This will help to ensure that you will have the latest cut of your information and data on hand. But if you use a private cloud, the advantage here is that you can literally "kill off" off those virtual machines (VMs) that have been created and create new ones in just a matter of a few minutes. Also, depending upon the plan that you have, you can even make copies of your VMs and store them in different datacenters around the world. So, if you are hit, you can just roll over to one of your backup datacenters and hardly experience any downtime.

6) *Always have security awareness training*:

This may sound like a broken record, but this is also crucial in fending off ransomware attacks. For instance, you may have the best lines of defense, but all it takes is one naïve employee to click on a malicious link for the malware to spread like wildfire. Therefore, it is more paramount than ever before to educate your employees on what to look out for. Also, keep in mind that if they are using company-issued devices to conduct their daily work tasks, as the employer, you have the right to conduct audits on these devices to make sure that they are being used in accordance with your security policy. But like conducting risk assessments, security awareness training is not a one-time deal either. You must hold these sessions regularly and even conduct simulated phishing attacks to see if your employees fall for the bait after they have received training.

7) *Always keep your computer updated*:

It is always important to keep your servers, computers, and even your wireless devices up to date with the latest software patches and upgrades. True, it may be a pain sometimes doing this (especially if you have the Windows 10 OS), but doing so will pay huge dividends in the end. Apart from this, there are also other preventative measures that you can take, which include the following:

- Always keep your Adobe Flash Player and other Java-based web browsers up to date as well. This will help to prevent any kind of "Exploit Kit" ransomware attacks from occurring.

- Disable the VSSADMIN.exe file:

  This is an obscure file in the Windows OS to administer what is known as the "Volume Shadow Copy Service". This is used to keep a version history of files in your computer that are not used very often or that are deemed to be arbitrary in nature. Since very few people actually use this tool, it has thus become a favored avenue of the cyberattacker.

- Disable the other automated services in the Windows OS. These include the following:

  → Script Host;

  → Power Shell;

  → Auto Play;

  → Remote Services.

8) *Shut down your entire computer system(s):*

If you think you may be in the beginning stages of a ransomware attack, immediately unplug your computer. This action will help to mitigate the actual. EXE file from entering your computer. However, if your IT infrastructure is large, shutting down the entire system is still your best bet. True, this will cause some downtime, inconvenience, and lost revenue, **but this cost is minimal** compared to if your business or corporation were to become an actual victim of a ransomware attack.

9) *Never, ever pay the cyberattacker:*

If in the unfortunate case that you do become a victim, **never pay the cyberattacker under any circumstances**. There are two primary reasons for this:

- Even if you do pay the ransom, there is no guarantee that you will get the decryption key with which to unlock your computer and files;

- Paying the cyberattacker will only fuel their motivation and greed to launch more ransomware attacks.

10) *Have more than one layer of authentication in place:*

Traditionally, it has been the password that has been used. But given how this can be easily hacked, many companies adopted what is known as "two factor authentication", or "2FA" for short. But even this too is falling short of providing any adequate level of protection, so now companies are adopting what is known as the "Zero Trust Framework". This is a methodology where absolutely nobody is trusted either internal or external to your organization, even your employees. Also, they must have to go through at least three or more layers of authentication, to absolutely confirm the legitimacy of their claims of who they are. This framework also implements multiple layers of security throughout your organization, each with their own set of authentication mechanisms in place. The thinking here is that if you are impacted by a ransomware attack, this will help to mitigate and contain its further spread.

11) *Use penetration testing:*

These are specific tests conducted with the main intent of totally breaking down your lines of defense, to discover where all the weak points, vulnerabilities, and back doors are in both your IT and network infrastructures. From here, recommendations are then provided as to how they can all be remediated as quickly as possible so that your organization does not fall prey to a ransomware attack. Also, you should consider seriously implementing threat hunting exercises as well, which probes to see if there is a cyberattacker actually lurking about your systems in a secretive fashion. Remember, the trend here is that they want to stay in for as long possible and inject malicious payload a bit at a time, so that the maximum amount of damage can be delivered. This is a topic that will be covered in more detail in Chapter 3 of this book.

Note

1 (Source: https://securityintelligence.com/news/ransomware-costs-expected-265-billion-2031/).

CHAPTER 2

A Technical Review of Ransomware Attacks

O UR LAST CHAPTER PROVIDED a detailed overview of the general concepts of ransomware. But one of the highlights of the chapter was how ransomware has evolved over time. It first started as something simple, but now it has become something that is almost a faceless giant. Given the interconnectedness of software and hardware today, ransomware can penetrate through just about everything, and worst yet, when you least expect it to happen.

Not only has the cyberattacker become extremely sophisticated and much more demanding in this regard, they also now take the time to study their targets. In other words, gone are the days of the traditional "Smash and Grab" campaigns with the main effort to steal anything and everything in plain sight. Now, the cyberattacker will use all the tools they have to profile their unsuspecting victims in order to truly discover their weak spots and vulnerabilities.

From here, once the moment is right, they will penetrate and stay for as long as they can inside the victim. This could be weeks, or even months, or perhaps in the worst-case scenario, even years. From here, the primary goal is to steal all the confidential information and data that is possible, but in a way that does not leave any indicators that something is wrong. Technically, this is known as "Data Exfiltration", and the victim will not know that anything has happened to them until it is too late.

DOI: 10.1201/9781003431633-3   **41**

From here, the cyberattacker can then launch extortion-style attacks, or even sell the personal identifiable information (PII) datasets on the Dark Web for a profit, or even hire out a third party to launch a ransomware as a Service attack. But the interesting thing here is that the cyberattacker is using tools that are publicly available to profile their targets, primarily using social media profiles (such as Twitter, LinkedIn, Facebook, etc.) and another tool called "Open Source Intelligence" (OSINT). This is becoming a favorite of the cyberattacker to carefully examine their victims in order to launch a ransomware attack. But what exactly is OSINT? The next subsection examines when OSINT is used for good purposes.

HOW TO USE OSINT

One of the best ways to use OSINT is for collecting information about your competition. In this regard, you can use this framework in four different ways, which are as follows:

- *Communications intelligence*:

  This is where to collect all sorts of information about your competition. Some of the best places to start are, of course, the company website, their social media sites, and any brochures that you can download. While many of these can be found easily by conducting a basic Google search, you will want to do a deeper dive as to what previous marketing campaigns looked like, as well as the past marketing collateral that was used. It would, of course, take a very long time to do this with traditional tools, but with the sophistication of OSINT, these can be found very quickly. With this past information, you can thus build a much-detailed profile about your competitor and try to use this to predict their future moves.

- *Financial intelligence*:

  This is probably one of the best clues that will tell you regarding what your competitor is planning next. Tools such as SEC filings, M and A activity, annual reports, etc. are publicly available. But what you really need to figure their next move is to get the detailed financial info. Determining where the particular assets are and what past liabilities looked like can you give you a really good clue. Finding this kind of information can relatively be easy for a publicly traded company but not for a private one, as data is closely held. So, what do you do in this situation? You can fall back on the breadth of OSINT to get as much information as you can, in order to start to paint their financial profile.

- *Technical intelligence*:

    In this instance, you want to gather as much data as you can about your competitor's product and service lines. Most of this can be found on their website, but what you really want is once again, that detailed information to figure what new products they are trying to come up with. For example, you will want to gain access to spec sheets, patents that they may hold, trademarks, etc. If you are trying to come up with a new product to stay ahead of the competition, it may not be necessary at all to find an entirely new one. You may just have to build a better mousetrap, and using the tools of OSINT can give you a much better access to getting this kind of detailed information.

- *Human intelligence*:

    This is the kind of information that can be gleaned only by talking directly to the employees of your competition and their customers. Obviously, the latter can prove to be the most difficult as many companies are not forthcoming with details about their client base, unless it is a client success that is posted on their website. So where can you get the "nitty gritty" on what your competitor's customers are saying about them? Once again, using the tools of OSINT will let you make this deep dive. Once you know what their customers are saying, you can then hit on these pain points and let them know how your company can help fill these needs that are being neglected.

CREATING THE RIGHT OSINT STRATEGY

As described, while OSINT can yield a ton of information that may not be found by doing Google searches, it is important that you come up with the right strategy to get the best results. Here are some tips to follow:

1) *Establish clear and measurable goals*:

    With this, you need to determine what kind of intelligence you need to collect. For example, is it a combination of all four categories, or just some of them? Also, what kind of time frame are you looking at in terms of data collection and analysis? Remember, this kind of data can go stale pretty quickly. Thus, it is imperative to set up a realistic timeline and put into action what you have learned and studied.

2) *Work with the right people*:

If you are not familiar with using the OSINT tools, you will need to hire somebody who can collect the information for you. But make sure that this is a person you absolutely trust, as you don't want them going to your competitor, which would defeat your whole fact-finding project altogether.

3) *Don't neglect the social media sites*:

Although the current line of thinking might be that these sources only provide only a limited amount of information, that is not true. You really need to comb through all the posts, videos, images, etc. to truly build up that profile on your competitor. The OSINT tools can quickly help you do this.

4) *Look at all the details*:

When you have collected the information, ask your OSINT consultant to help you go over every detail of it. In a way, it's like data mining. The most important trends are those that are not noticed and buried deep underneath. The same is true here; remember that old proverb, "the devil is in the details".

But in the end, no matter what tools the cyberattacker uses to launch a ransomware attack, serious damage is done to the victim; not only does it take a toll financially, but it can also take quite a long time to recover from. In the last chapter, we examined some real-world examples of ransomware attacks. But in this chapter, we take a deeper dive by looking at more of them, and at the end, special attention is given to one in particular – the infamous SolarWinds attack.

MORE REAL-WORLD EXAMPLES OF RANSOMWARE ATTACKS

Here is the listing:

1) *WannaCry:*

Characteristics	Details
Kind of Attack	Crypto Ransomware
Year of Launch	2017
Cyberattacker Group	The Shadow Brokers
Victims	All end users that used any version of the Windows operating system (over 250,000 victims in 150 countries)
Financial Loss	$4 billion
Current State	Still deemed to be active, but the Decryption Keys are now available

Other details:

WannaCry has become dormant because of a researcher in the United Kingdom by the name of Marcus Hutchins. The domain hosting the malware was registered as a domain in the source code that made up the malware.

2) *TeslaCrypt:*

Characteristics	Details
Kind of Attack	Trojan Horse/Crypto Ransomware
Year of Launch	2015
Cyberattacker Group	Not known
Victims	All end users that used any version of the Windows XP, 7, and 8 operating systems
Financial Loss	$500 per end user
Current State	Dormant since 2016

Other details:

This ransomware hit over 185 gaming files, such as the Call of Duty series, World of Warcraft, Minecraft, World of Tanks, etc. It captured all the PI datasets of the end user as they were playing these online games.

There were over four different versions of this, and the last one could encrypt files up to 4GB in size.

3) *NotPetya*:

Characteristics	Details
Kind of Attack	Ransomware
Year of Launch	2017
Cyberattacker Group	Sandworm
Victims	Businesses in the EU (most notably those of Ukraine, France, and Germany)
Financial Loss	$10 billion
Current State	Can remerge again, but the Decryption Keys are now available

Other details:

This ransomware infected the master boot record of Windows operating system to take over the devices. A backdoor was created during the creation of a software update from the Ukrainian company known as "M.E. Doc".

4) *Sodinokibi*:

Characteristics	Details
Kind of Attack	Ransomware
Year of Launch	2019
Cyberattacker Group	REvil
Victims	JBS and Kaseya
Financial Loss	$200 million
Current State	Can remerge again, but the Decryption Keys are now available

Other details:

The following file extensions were primarily targeted:

• .jpg	• .3dm	• .dxf	• .rb	• .prel
• .jpeg	• .max	• .cpp	• .java	• .aet
• .raw	• accdb	• .cs	• .aaf	• .ppj
• .tif	• .db	• .h	• .aep	• .gif
• .png	• .mdb	• .php	• .aepx	• .psd
• .bmp	• .dwg	• .asp	• .plb	

5) *SamSam*:

Characteristics	Details
Kind of Attack	Locker
Year of Launch	2018
Cyberattacker Group	SamSam
Victims	Any kind or type of United States using the Windows operating system
Financial Loss	$6 million
Current State	Still Active

Other details:

This particular ransomware exploited the weaknesses and vulnerabilities in the various Windows servers to establish real-time access to the entire network infrastructure. As a result, the cyberattackers infected the entire network infrastructure and encrypted all the other servers that resided in it.

6) *Colonial Pipeline*:

Characteristics	Details
Kind of Attack	Locker
Year of Launch	2021
Cyberattacker Group	DarkSide
Victims	The Colonial Pipeline Company
Financial Loss	$4.4 million
Current State	Ransom was paid to stop further spread of the malware

Other details:

On May 7, 2021, Colonial Pipeline was forced to shut down operations across 17 states. A ransom payment of 75 Bitcoin (equivalent to $4.4 million) was paid with the assistance of the FBI. They were able to recover around $2.3 million from the ransom payment.

7) *Kronos attack*:

Characteristics	Details
Kind of Attack	Crypto
Year of Launch	2021
Cyberattacker Group	Not known
Victims	The Kronos Group
Financial Loss	Not known
Current State	Ransom was paid to stop further spread of the malware

Other details:

This ransomware impacted the Kronos Private Cloud. A lot of victims lost crucial employment-related data. Although the ransom was paid, there are still many lawsuits that were filed and need to be resolved.

8) *Impressa attack*:

Characteristics	Details
Kind of Attack	Locker
Year of Launch	2022
Cyberattacker Group	Lapsus$
Victims	The entire Impressa Company
Financial Loss	Not known
Current State	Ransomware was stopped

Other details:

The cyberattacker group heisted the entire IT and network infrastructure of Impressa. Although the attack was stopped, they still have full control over the social media sites of Impressa.

9) *The government of Costa Rica*:

Characteristics	Details
Kind of Attack	Locker
Year of Launch	2022
Cyberattacker Group	Conti Group
Victims	30 Agencies of the Costa Rican Government
Financial Loss	$30 million per day
Current State	Deemed to be still active

Other details:

This kind of ransomware attack was identified as an act of war by the pro-Russiaan Conti group. The Costa Rican Government is still recovering, with steep financial losses.

10) *The Swissport attack*:

Characteristics	Details
Kind of Attack	Crypto
Year of Launch	2022
Cyberattacker Group	BlackCat
Victims	The Swissport Company
Financial Loss	Not known
Current State	Ransomware halted, but over 1.6 Terabytes of information and data were stolen, not yet recovered

Other details:

The Swissport Company has a presence in 310 airports and over 50 countries. Despite this global dominance, the damage from the Ransomware attack was fairly minimal.

(SOURCE: www.getastra.com/blog/security-audit/
biggest-ransomware-attacks/)

THE SOLARWINDS ATTACK

Apart from the other kinds and types of ransomware attacks in this chapter and the last one, the SolarWinds ransomware attack is still probably one of the most well-known. This was deemed to be a "supply chain attack". A technical definition of it is as follows:

> A supply chain attack is a type of cyberattack that targets a trusted third-party vendor who offers services or software vital to the supply chain.
>
> Software supply chain attacks inject malicious code into an application in order to infect all users of an app, while hardware supply chain attacks compromise physical components for the same purpose.
>
> (SOURCE: www.crowdstrike.com/cybersecurity-101/
> cyberattacks/supply-chain-attacks/)

Simply put, this is where a cyberattacker inserts a malicious payload into a vulnerability of a third-party software. This typically happens in software upgrades and patches. As the end users eventually download them, they become infected with this malicious payload. So, the cyberattacker uses just one point of entry to infect thousands of unsuspecting victims. This is illustrated in the following diagram:

The next subsections will do a deep dive into the anatomy of the SolarWinds ransomware attack.

WHAT ACTUALLY HAPPENED – SOLARWINDS

First, SolarWinds is a rather large software company that creates and deploys network monitoring tools. These are primarily used by larger companies in corporate America, especially by managed service providers (MSPs) that keep an eye on the IT and network infrastructures for their clients.

Through this, any sort or type of anomalies can be detected in the network flow of traffic, and any corrective actions can be taken immediately, which is often done remotely. One of these tools that is manufactured by SolarWinds is known as "Orion".

It is important to note at this point that this kind of hack is different from the others that we are accustomed to hearing about. Specifically, this is known as a "supply chain attack". This simply means that rather than breaking into digital assets of SolarWinds, other third parties that used the Orion software package were targeted.

With this kind of approach, the cyberattacker was thus able to breach into the lines of defense of many other private and public entities.

For example, in this situation, over 30,000 entities were impacted globally. Now the question is what was the main point of entry by which all this havoc was created? Well, back in December 2020, many of SolarWinds' customers that used Orion already had deployed two major software updates to it.

But what were thought to be system patches were actually pieces of nefarious malware, disguised to look like legitimate and safe downloads.

Even more bewildering is the fact that the cyberattackers already had gained access to the software development platforms that created these updates going back as far as October 2019. They were able to access them through the gaps and vulnerabilities that were present in the many Microsoft Office 365 that the employees of SolarWinds used daily.

So, once the cyberattackers were in and were able to stay that way without going unnoticed, they then examined some of the best ways in which they could cause the maximum amount of damage that was possible. They determined that inserting Trojan Horses into these platforms would be the best way to accomplish this goal.

So, in March 2020, the insertion of these malicious payloads started to take place, which would be known as "SUNBURST". But apart from this, the cyberattackers also created various backdoors in these payloads that would communicate with third-party servers over which they had control over.

From here, any personal identifiable information (PII) datasets of both employees and customers could be covertly hijacked and either be sold on the Dark Web for a rather nice profit or be used to launch subsequent identity theft attacks.

But what was even worse is that these malicious payloads, backdoors, and Trojan Horses appeared to be legitimate modifications to the software patches and upgrades that were ultimately downloaded by the many business and government entities that used the Orion system.

Now, the next question is how could this level of believability be established, and why did it take so long to discover?

Well, the various types of malicious payloads were inserted into the "SolarWinds.Orion.Core.BusinessLayer.dll". These are the dynamic link libraries (DLLs) that were created for the software patches and upgrades exclusively for Orion. To get through, these DLLs were signed by digital certificates that verified their authenticity but were also covertly tampered with.

To make matters even worse, these DLLs were designed to be dormant for a period of 14 days, so that any confidential information could be easily transmitted back to the third-party servers.

THE TIMELINE OF THE ATTACK – SOLARWINDS[1]

It is important to note that the SolarWinds security breach did not happen just all at once. Rather, there was a lot of thought and planning put forth by the cyberattackers, as the following timeline demonstrates.

From the Standpoint of the Cyberattackers

September 4, 2019:

The cyberattackers gain the first known foothold into the SolarWinds IT and network infrastructures.

September 12, 2019:

The cyberattacker group deploys the first malicious payload into the Orion Software platform. This was deemed to be just a test run, as the hackers used numerous servers located in various parts of the US to cover their network tracks.

February 20, 2020:

The cyberattackers do a second test run of the malicious payload to make sure that it will cause the damage that it was created to do.

June 4, 2020:

The test code is removed again so that it cannot be detected. After this second trial run, it appears all is working properly.

From the Standpoint of SolarWinds

December 8, 2020:

Fire Eye, one of the world's leading cybersecurity firms, made it known to the public that its IT and network infrastructures were hacked into and that the cyberattackers even did away with its Red Teaming penetration tools.

December 11, 2020:

Fire Eye also makes the discovery that SolarWinds had also been compromised, to a great degree. The realization that this was actually a supply chain style attack came when Fire Eye further discovered that Orion Platform, which was used to deploy the software updates, was also hacked into between the time frame of March 2020 and June 2020.

December 12, 2020:

Fire Eye formally notifies SolarWinds that their Orion Platform has been the vehicle for deploying the malware, through the software upgrades and patches. At this time also, the National Security Council of the US federal government also intervenes to ascertain if any agencies had been impacted by this cyberattack.

From the Standpoint of the American Public

December 13, 2020:

A number of key events occurred on this date, which are as follows:

- The Cybersecurity and Infrastructure Security Agency (CISA) requires that all US federal government agencies discontinue use of the Orion Platform immediately.

- SolarWinds releases temporary fixes that the impacted entities could use to mitigate the risk of further damage taking place.

- Fire Eye makes this cyberattack officially a supply chain hack, because other third parties were also impacted, namely some of the largest companies in the Fortune 500.

- Microsoft also intervenes and explains to the public how its customer base could be impacted by this cyberattack.

- The hack makes the news wires for the first time, with finger pointing and blame being at nation state threat actors.

From the Standpoint of Risk Mitigation

December 15, 2020:

Key events transpired on this date, which are as follows:

- SolarWinds releases the first software fixes to further mitigate the damage that has already been done.

- The first victims have been identified.

- The CISA and the FBI launch joint efforts to determine how the SolarWinds breach occurred in the first place and to further investigate the damage that has been done to US federal government agencies.

THE VICTIMS OF THE ATTACK – SOLARWINDS

Recent reports peg the total number at about 18,000 individual victims, which were primarily employees. Over 40 business entities were impacted, and according to Microsoft, 44% of these were technology-related companies. Here is a listing of companies that were hit:

- US Department of Commerce;

- Department of Defense;

- Department of Energy;

- Department of Homeland Security;

- Department of State;

- Department of the Treasury;

- Department of Health;

- Microsoft;

- Intel;

- Cisco;

- Nvidia;

- VMware;

- Belkin;
- FireEye;
- Cisco;
- Deloitte;
- Mount Sinai Hospital;
- Ciena;
- NCR;
- SAP;
- Intel;
- Digital Sense;
- Stratus Networks;
- City of Page;
- Christie Clinic Telehealth;
- Res Group;
- City of Barrie;
- TE Connectivity;
- The Fisher Barton Group;
- South Davis Community Hospital;
- College of Law and Business, Israel;
- Magnolia Independent School District;
- Fidelity Communications;
- Stingray;
- Keyano College;
- NSW Health;
- City of Kingston, Ontario, Canada;
- Ironform;

- Digital Sense;

- Signature Bank;

- PQ Corporation;

- BancCentral Financial Services Corporation;

- Kansas City Power and Light Company;

- SM Group;

- CYS Group;

- William Osler Health System;

- W. R. Berkley Insurance Australia;

- Dufferin County, Ontario, Canada;

- City of Farmington;

- Newton Public Schools;

- Stearns Bank;

- Ville de Terrebonne;

- Hamilton Company

- Cosgroves;

- City of Moncton;

- Mediatek;

- Capilano University;

- City of Prince George;

- Community Options for Families & Youth;

- IES Communications;

- Saskatoon Public Schools;

- Regina Public Schools;

- Public Hospitals Authority, Caribbean;

- INSEAD Business School;

- DenizBank;

- Bisco International;

- IDSolutions;

- Arizona Arthritis & Rheumatology Associates;

- Optimizely;

- Aerion Corporation;

- Pima County, Arizona;

- City of Sacramento;

- Clinica Sierra Vista;

- Sana Biotechnology;

- Ecobank;

- Helix Water District;

- Lukoil;

- Mutual of Omaha Bank;

- NeoPhotonics Corporation;

- Samuel Merritt University;

- College of the Siskiyous;

- Vantage Data Centers;

- Vocera Communications.

THE LESSONS LEARNED FROM THE ATTACK – SOLARWINDS

Given the large scope of this breach, there are many key takeaways an IT Security can apply, but the following are some of the big ones:

1) *Always know where your source code is coming from:*

As previously discussed, the malicious payload was inserted into the various dynamic link libraries (DDLs) and then masqueraded as a legitimate software software/upgrade to the Orion Platform. In this instance, it is unlikely that any kind of tests were conducted in the source code of the software to make sure that there was no malware in them before they were deployed onto the customer's IT/network infrastructure. Had this been done, it is quite probable that this kind of attack could have been stopped in its tracks, or at the very least, the damage that it created could have been contained. Therefore, it is crucial that CISOs take a proactive approach in testing all forms of source code (for example, whether it is used in creating a web app or software patch) to remediate any gaps and vulnerabilities before they are released out to the production environment.

2) *Vetting of third parties:*

The SolarWinds security breach has been technically referred to as a "supply chain attack". This simply means that the cyberattackers took advantage of the vulnerabilities of third parties that SolarWinds used, in order to inflict the maximum damage possible. This underscores the importance of one of the most basic rules: always vet your suppliers before you hire and onboard one. This means that as a CISO, you need to make sure that your IT Security is carefully scrutinizing the security procedures and policies of that particular third party that you are thinking of outsourcing some of your business functions to. It must be part of what you have in place in your organization, or even better than that. But simply making sure of what your potential supplier has put into place in terms of controls is not a one-time deal. Even after you have hired and have a business relationship with them, you need to make sure that they are strictly enforcing these controls regularly. This can take place by conducting a security audit. In the end, if your supplier becomes a victim of a cyberattack and the personal identifiable information (PII) datasets you have entrusted are breached, ***you will be held legally and financially responsible, not them***.

3) *Keep things simple and easy to track:*

It is simply human nature to think that investing in a large amount of security tools and technologies means that you will be immune from a security breach. But in reality, this is far from the truth. In fact, taking this proverbial "Safety in Numbers" approach simply expands the attack surface for the hacker, which was experienced in the SolarWinds breach. Instead, it is far wiser to invest in perhaps five firewalls versus ten of them, but make sure that they are strategically deployed to where they are needed the most. By using this kind of methodology, not only will your IT Security Team be able to filter out those threats that are real, but you will also be able to pinpoint the entry point of the cyberattacker much more quickly, versus the time it took SolarWinds, simply due to the fact of the overload of tools and technologies they had in place. Because of this, and as previously discussed, it took months before anybody realized that something was wrong. In this regard, you may even want to use both artificial intelligence (AI) and machine learning (ML) tools. With this kind of automation in place, false positives will be a thing of the past, and those alerts and warnings that are legitimate and for real will be triaged and escalated much more quickly.

4) *Use segmentation*:

In today's environment, many businesses are now seriously considering adopting what is known as the Zero Trust Framework. This is the kind of methodology where absolutely nobody is trusted in both the internal and external environments. Further, any individual wishing to gain access to a particular shared resource must be verified through at least three or more layers of authentication. But apart from this, another critical component of this is the creation of "Subnets". With this, you are breaking up your entire network infrastructure into smaller ones. But what is key here is that each of these Subnets has its own layer of defense, so it becomes almost statistically impossible for a cyberattacker to break through every layer. SolarWinds did not take this approach with their network infrastructure, so as a result, the cyberattackers were able to get in through the first time around.

5) *Update your security technologies*:

With the advent of the remote workforce, the traditional security tools such as the virtual private network (VPN) have started to reach their breaking points, and thus their defensive capabilities. Because of this, it is important that you consider upgrading these systems to what is known as the Next Generation Firewall. These kinds of technologies are now becoming much more robust in ascertaining malicious data packets that are both entering and leaving your network infrastructure. SolarWinds did not invest properly in these kinds of upgrades, so therefore, the cyberattackers were able to penetrate through the weaknesses of the VPNs that they were using.

THE LESSONS LEARNED FROM THE SOLARWINDS RANSOMWARE ATTACK

Upon a closer examination of this list of victims, one can see that this truly represents a cross section of industries. For example, public, private, educational, government agencies (on both the federal and local levels), and even nonprofit centers were heavily impacted.

It is important to keep in mind that many of the organizations listed here may not have been hit directly, but rather, they were hit indirectly because of the cascading nature of this security breach.

But nonetheless, this list clearly demonstrates that the SolarWinds attack has been deemed to be one of the largest in the world, and attacks like this or even worse are likely to occur and occur again until a proactive mind-set is completely enforced with CISOs and IT Security Teams on a worldwide basis.

The financial damage caused by the SolarWinds breach is now up to $90 million, and it is estimated that it could even reach as high as $100 billion when all is said and done.

In the end, whenever a cyberattack hits any business entity, no matter how large or small, it is always very important to reconstruct a detailed timeline like this one. The primary advantage of this is that it can aid in the process of attribution, which determines who the actual perpetrators are.

Also, it can pinpoint those areas in which latent evidence may lie, which is very crucial in carrying out the forensics investigation.

RANSOMWARE AND CRITICAL INFRASTRUCTURE

As it has been mentioned in Chapter 1, most of the previous ransomware attacks have been targeting the digital infrastructure of the United States and other countries around the world. But now, a new trend is emerging, and that is now using ransomware to target the critical infrastructure. Technically, it can be defined as follows:

Critical infrastructure includes the vast network of highways, connecting bridges and tunnels, railways, utilities and buildings necessary to maintain normalcy in daily life. Transportation, commerce, clean water and electricity all rely on these vital systems.

(SOURCE: www.dhs.gov/science-and-technology/
critical-infrastructure)

An illustration of this is next:

Although anything in this regard can be considered a target, the ones that could have the most detrimental impact upon our society are ransomware attacks to the water supply lines, oil and natural gas (like the Colonial Pipeline attack), nuclear facilities, and even our food distribution system from the farm all the way down to the consumer. The following subsections provide more insight into ransomware attacks on the critical infrastructure of the United States.

THE TOP FIVE RANSOMWARE ATTACKS ON THE CRITICAL INFRASTRUCTURE

1) *Attacks on the power grids in Ukraine*:

This occurred in December 2015. The electric grid still used the traditional Supervisory Control and Data Acquisition (SCADA) system, which was not upgraded for the longest time. This cyberattack impacted about 230,000 residents in that area, who were without power for a few hours. Although this threat variant was short-lived, it further illustrates the grave weaknesses of the critical infrastructure. For example, the traditional spear phishing E-mail was used to launch the threat vector, and in fact just a year later, the same E-mail was used to attack an electrical substation near Kiev, causing major blackouts for a long period of time.

2) *Attack on the water supply lines in New York*:

The target this time was the Rye Brook Water Dam. Although the actual Infrastructure was small in comparison, there were lasting repercussions. The primary reason for this is that this was one of the first instances in which a nation state actor was actually blamed, and all fingers pointed toward Iran. The most surprising facet of this cyberattack was that it occurred in 2013 but was not reported to the public until 2016. Even more striking is that the malicious threat actors were able to gain access to the command center of these facilities by using just an ordinary dial up modem.

3) *Impacts to the ACH system*:

Although the global financial system may not directly fit into the classical definition of a critical infrastructure, the impacts felt by any cyberattack can be just as great. In this threat variant, it was the SWIFT Global Messaging system that was the primary target. This is used by banks and other money institutions to provide details about the electronic movement of money, which includes ACH, wire transfers, etc. This is a heavily used system worldwide, as almost 34 million electronic transfers use this particular infrastructure. The Lazarus cyberattack group, originating from North Korea, were able to gain a foothold into the banks by using hijacked SWIFT login username and password combinations. This attack is one of the first of its kind in the international banking sector.

4) *Damages to nuclear facilities*:

Probably one of the well-known cyberattacks on this kind of infrastructure was upon the Wolf Creek Nuclear Operating Corporation, which is in Kansas. In this instance, spear phishing E-mails were leveraged against key personnel working at these facility, who had specific control and access to the controls at this nuclear facility.

Although the extent of the damage has been kept classified, this situation clearly demonstrates the vulnerability of the US-based nuclear facilities. For example, if a cyberattacker were to gain access into one, they could move laterally to other nuclear power plants, causing damage in a cascading style, with the same or even greater effects of a thermonuclear war.

5) *Attack on the water supply*:

The most well-known attack just happened recently in Oldsmar, Florida. Although the details of this cyberattack are still coming to light, it has been suspected that the hacker was able to gain control by using a remote access tool, such as Team Viewer. But there were other grave weaknesses in the infrastructure as well, such as a very outdated operating system (OS) and very poor password enforcement (such as not creating long and complex ones and rotating them out frequently). In this instance, the goal of the cyberattacker was not just to cause damage to the water supply system, but also to even gravely affect the health of the residents who drank the water, by poisoning it with a chemical-based lye. Luckily, an employee was able to quickly notice what was going on and immediately reversed the settings that were put into motion by the cyberattacker. However, it is still not known yet whether this hack occurred outside US soil or from within. If it is the latter, then this will raise even more alarm bells that domestic-based cyberattackers are just as much of a grave threat as the nation state actors to our critical infrastructure.

THE CYBER RISKS THAT CAN AFFECT AN ICS

Just like in the digital and virtual worlds, there are numerous threats that can affect the industrial control systems (ICS) of any type or kind of critical infrastructure. Some of these are as follows:

1) *Air gapping will no longer work*:

As it was reviewed earlier, many pieces that make up a critical infrastructure were built in the late 1970s to early 1980s. Because of how long they have remained in place, one cannot just rip out these old pieces and put new ones back in place. Back then, of course, the threat of cyberattacks was not even a concern. The main point of contention was physical access entry. For example, what if an impostor was able to gain entry and misconfigure any settings? Or what if there was a rogue employee intent on launching an insider attack? One of the biggest security measures that could be afforded during those times is "air gapping". In a way, this is very similar to dividing up your IT/network infrastructure into different regimes, also known as "Subnets". With air gapping, the ICS network was completely isolated from the rest of the critical infrastructure. The theory was that if an Insider Attack were launched, any effects from it would not be transmitted down to the ICS. But even now, air gapping is not a feasible solution to protect against cyberattacks. The primary reason for this is that both the physical and digital/virtual worlds are now coming together and being joined as one whole unit through a phenomenon called the "Industrial Internet of Things" (IIoT). Because of this, trying to protect the ICS is now proving to be a very difficult task, because once again, you simply cannot put in a new security system to protect it. Rather, they have to be added on as separate components, but the key is that each one of them must be interoperable with the legacy ICS network.

2) *Legacy hardware and software components*:

Because of the major difficulties in finding the right security tools to add on, many critical infrastructures are still using outdated hardware and software components. Among the most at risk to a cyberattack are the following:

- Programmable logic controllers (PLCs);

- Remote terminal units (RTUs);

- Distributed control systems (DCSs).

The aforementioned devices are typically used to manage the processes as well as the sub-processes of the ICS network. Because of the lack of cyber threats back then, these pieces hardware and software were not built with any sort of authentication mechanism, or even encryption. In fact, even to this day, these components are more than likely not protected. As a result, anybody who can network access to the critical infrastructure could move laterally and gain access to these particular devices, and literally shut them off within minutes. The result would be quite disastrous. For example, the flow of water, oil and natural gas, and even electricity could come to a grinding halt almost instantaneously, taking months to restore them back to their normal working conditions. In fact, in this situation, a cyberattacker does not even have to be at the physical premises of the critical infrastructure. Since the flow of network communications is done in a clear text format from within the ICS network, a cyberattacker could be literally on the other side of the world and deliver their malicious payload, say, to an oil refinery in the southern United States. But worst yet, many of the operating systems (OSs) that are used in critical infrastructure are totally outdated and no longer supported by Microsoft. These include the likes of Windows NT and Windows XP. Also unfortunately, given the legacy structure of an ICS network, the IT departments at many critical infrastructures are typically far more concerned about maintaining the stability of their IT/network infrastructure. They take the view that any attempt to patch the components just described will simply result in unnecessary downtime or unexpected halts to critical operations, which cannot be afforded at all costs.

3) *There is no clear-cut visibility*:

One of the greatest advantages of using a cloud-based solution like the AWS or Microsoft Azure is that they can let you see inside your infrastructure with 100% visibility, thus letting you track down any sort of malicious activity that is taking place. But this is the total opposite of an ICS, which offers no visibility; thus as a result, it is almost too hard to detect if there is any suspicious behavior that is transpiring until it is way too late. Because of this, many of the settings in an ICS are difficult to configure properly in order to meet today's demand for the basic utility necessities of the everyday American.

4) *The communications protocols are outdated*:

With the remote workforce today, the talk of various network protocols has now come into almost daily conversation. For example, most people have heard of TCP/IP, IPsec, 5G wireless networks, etc. For the most part, the communication channels of these various protocols can operate together, to some degree or another, with virtually minimal downtime, if any. But this is not the case with ICS networks. Each one of them is outdated as well as proprietary in nature, developed decades ago. For example, this is most prevalent in the so-called control-layer protocols that are used. Because of this, this is yet another backdoor for the cyberattacker to enter. For example, the mathematical logic that is implemented into the hardware of the ICS can be rather easily changed around, thus resulting in an unintentional flow in mission critical operations.

WHAT IS SCADA?

A Supervisory Control and Data Acquisition (SCADA) system is an automated control system that is used primarily in critical infrastructure. This includes areas such as the following:

- Energy;
- Gas and oil;
- Water;
- Electricity grid;
- Nuclear facilities;
- Power plants;
- Food and agricultural processors.

Because of the gravity of these applications, a SCADA system will be on the target list for the cyberattacker. For example, multiple cities across the United States can be impacted, with multiple outages occurring at gas stations, electrical power plants, water supply lines, etc. In other words, our lives will come to a complete halt.

THE CYBERSECURITY ISSUES OF SCADA

There are key security issues with SCADA, and the major ones are as follows:

- *Outdated technologies:*

  Many of the SCADA systems that are in use today were deployed several years ago. Back then, cybersecurity was barely an issue, so more consideration was given to physical security controls. The major concern now is that the SCADA system will be used as a point of entry to launch an attack on a critical infrastructure.

- *Open visibility*:

  Because SCADA systems were deployed so long ago, the actual physical layout as to where they would reside within a business was not considered. As a result of this, many systems are open, and because of that, there are greater chances of an insider attack. There is a growing awareness in this aspect, and businesses that use SCADA are trying to put advanced physical controls in place to protect it. But the main problem is that these newer technologies have to be added onto the existing legacy security system that is in place. There can be interoperability issues with this, thus creating more gaps and weaknesses in an already fragile environment.

- *Network integration*:

  SCADA systems were designed to operate by themselves, meaning any future integration into other technologies was not even considered. With the advent of the Internet of Things (IoT), everything is now interconnected with each other, even the SCADA systems. Once again, there are interoperability issues that are coming out, and this increased interlinking is also expanding the attack surface for the cyberattacker.

In fact, just recently, one of the customers of Schneider Electric experienced a cyberattack on their SCADA system. In this instance, the cyberattacker(s) took complete advantage of a vulnerability within the firmware that was used, and from there was able to launch a zero-day privilege escalation attack. This allowed them to gain control of the entire emergency shutdown process.

Other attacks on SCADA systems include the following:

- In March of 2018, a cyberattack disrupted the power lines that fed into the natural gas pipelines all across the United States;

- In June of 2016, malware was discovered on the IT/network infrastructure of a major energy company based in Europe. This led to covert backdoors being created in the SCADA system with the result being that the entire European energy grid could have been shut down.

HOW TO ADDRESS THE SECURITY ISSUES
OF A SCADA SYSTEM

The main issue with SCADA systems is that a bulk of them were built in the 1970s and 1980s. Because of this, and the dependency that we have upon it today, you simply cannot "rip out" the old and put in newer technology to secure it. Rather, you have to find those security tools that can be added on to the legacy architecture that is already in place.

But in the end, it is still possible to secure SCADA systems, and here are some ways in which it can be done:

1) Correctly ascertain all the connections to the SCADA system. This is like conducting a risk assessment for an IT/network infrastructure.

2) Based on the aforementioned, if there are any connections that are deemed to be unnecessary, disconnect them all at once. This is like disabling service ports when they are not being used.

3) For the remaining connections, make sure that they are hardened to the greatest extent possible.

4) Although SCADA systems have been built with proprietary technologies that are not designed to commingle with others, do not further implement any proprietary protocols. It is crucial at this point that everything works together.

5) If possible, run a penetration test or even a threat hunting test to see if there are any hidden backdoors in the system. Remember, the cyberattacker of today is looking for these all the time as an easy and covert way to get entry.

6) It is important to deploy firewalls, network intrusion devices, and routers, etc. surrounding the SCADA system so that you can be notified in real time of any potential security breaches that may be happening. Also, use a 24 x 7 x 365 incident monitoring tool.

7) Regularly conduct risk assessments and audits of all internal and remote devices that are connected to the SCADA system.

8) Like a penetration test, formulate a "Red Team" so that you can tear down the walls of defense to ascertain where all known and unknown vulnerabilities and gaps lie. From there, it is absolutely crucial that these are remedied as quickly as possible.

9) Again, just as you would for your IT/network infrastructure, it is important to define roles and responsibilities regarding who will actually "protect" the SCADA system. For example, this will include those individuals who are responsible for downloading and deploying the security patches and upgrades, responding to a cyberattack that is targeted toward it, and bringing the system back up and running after the threat vector has been mitigated.

10) Create, deploy, and strictly enforce a data backup policy, as well as an incident response/disaster recovery (IR/DR) plan, and make sure that these are routinely practiced. For example, data should be backed up daily (perhaps even every few hours), and the IR/DR plan should be rehearsed quarterly.

WHAT THE FUTURE HOLDS – RANSOMWARE AND THE CRITICAL INFRASTRUCTURE

Cyberattacks on critical infrastructure are occurring at a more rapid rate now, and it has garnered the attention of the industry. However, it has not yet fully captured the sense of urgency in that something needs to be done to further fortify these structures. What is anticipated for the future? Here is a glimpse:

1) *Segmentation could occur*:

In the digital world, this is one of the big buzzwords that is being floated around right now. At the present time, most businesses typically have just one line of defense that separates the threats from the external environment into the internal environment. This is very often referred to as "perimeter security". But the basic flaw (and a very serious one) is that once the cyberattacker is able to break through this, they can pretty much move laterally and get access to anything they want. Thus, with the implementation of MFA and the Zero Trust Framework, there have been calls now to further divide up the IT and network infrastructure that exists in the internal environment into smaller chunks, and this is known as "segmentation". Each segment would have its own set of defenses, and the statistical probability of a cyberattacker breaking through all these segments becomes lower every time, and as a result, they give up in frustration. It is hoped that this same line of thinking can also be applied to critical infrastructure, but the main problem once again is that they all consist of legacy computer systems, which may or may not support the segmentation efforts. Even if they do, there is no guarantee that it will be sustainable in the long term.

2) *The Internet of Things*:

Right now, this phenomenon has been further catapulted by the rise of the remote workforce, where pretty much everything has gone digital. This is the notion where all the objects that we interact with in both virtual and physical worlds are interconnected. There is great interest in IoT and even efforts are currently being undertaken to bring the world of the IoT into critical infrastructure. This now becomes known as the "Industrial Internet of Things", or "IIoT" for short. But it is expected that this trend will quickly dissipate into the future, as more cybersecurity attacks are launched against critical infrastructure. The reason for this is simple: with an IIoT in place, the attack surface becomes much greater, and the number of backdoors that the cyberattacker can penetrate is now greatly multiplied.

3) *The financial damage will escalate*:

As more threat vectors are launched, they will obviously become more sophisticated and covert in nature. Given this, the financial toll that it will take on critical infrastructure that is impacted is expected to reach well over the multimillion-dollar mark. It is anticipated that the downtime period to recover from future attacks will be a lot longer than what it is at the present time, thus adding more to the financial toll. Also, with the convergence that is currently taking place within the IT and the operational technology (OT) realms, the cyberattacker will be able to easily gain access to either the ICS or SCADA systems via any vulnerabilities or gaps that still persist in the network of the critical infrastructure.

4) *A closer collaboration with cybersecurity*:

It is also expected that the leaders of critical infrastructure will start to work closely with the cybersecurity industry. Not only will there be attempts made to try to add on security tools/technologies that can interoperate with the legacy ones, but there will even be a greater effort to share threat intelligence information/date on a real-time basis so the IT Security Teams of critical infrastructure can be much better prepared to handle any threat vectors that are looming on the horizon. This new movement has been appropriately termed the era of "Shared Responsibility".

5) *A greater need for cybersecurity insurance*:

Essentially, by purchasing this kind of policy, a company in theory can be protected by financial losses if they are impacted by a cyber-attack. But the reality holds different in the sense that there is still a lot of confusion out there as to what will technically be covered. So, while a company may think they have full coverage, the chances are that they will not get a 100% payout. But despite this, the critical infrastructure is starting to understand the need for some sort of financial protection in case they are breached. Thus, there will be a great increase in demand for cybersecurity insurance policies in the coming years, to recoup any financial damages incurred by attacks to legacy systems.

6) *A migration to the cloud*:

At the present time, there are a lot of efforts to move on premises solutions to a cloud-based platform, such as the AWS or Microsoft Azure. While there could be some success with this as it relates to critical infrastructure, there is also the realization that a pure 100% migration will probably not happen. The primary reason for this is that once again, most of the technologies for critical infrastructure were developed back in the 70s and the 80s. Thus, trying to put all of this into something as advanced as the cloud probably will not occur.

Overall, this chapter has reviewed in great detail examples of more ransomware attacks. It should be noted that the height of the ransomware attacks peaked during the height of the COVID-19 pandemic. During this time, the main goal of humanity was just pure survival, and because of that cybersecurity took a back seat when compared to the other pressing issues at hand.

But since then, the number of ransomware attacks have declined. While that is good news for sure, the bad news is that ransomware as a threat will persist in our society for a very long time. Now the biggest fear, as stated before, is a colossal ransomware attack on multiple United States cities all at once, with a primary focus on our critical infrastructure.

It will take weeks and possibly even months to recover from this kind of large-scale attack. American citizens simply could not survive for that long of a time frame. In the next chapter, we will focus on areas that can greatly help reduce the chances of being impacted by a ransomware attack. This is known as penetration testing.

Note

1 (Source: https://platform.keesingtechnologies.com/the-solarwinds-hack-part-2/).

CHAPTER 3

The Importance of Penetration Testing

S O FAR IN THIS book, Chapter 1 had provided an overview into ransomware and its evolution. Other areas of ransomware were explored and reviewed as well. Chapter 2 did a deeper look into examples of some of the top ransomware attacks over the last couple of decades. There was also a special focus aimed at the vulnerabilities and weaknesses of the critical infrastructure of the United States.

The reason why so much attention was given to this aspect of the cyber threat landscape is that these are traditionally legacy-based systems – meaning, most of the technologies that were used to create the components of the critical infrastructure were done back in the 1960s and 1970s. During this time frame, the thought of a cybersecurity attack impacting them was never even heard of. The term "cybersecurity" was not even coined then either. The main threats to the critical infrastructure at the time were all about unauthorized access to the particular facilities.

This is an area known as "physical access entry", and it still dominates today's threat landscape, even though cybersecurity has pervaded the news headlines daily. Now, the main issue with regard to critical infrastructure is how to make them more secure. The main problem here is that since these systems are so old and outdated, one cannot simply rip out the old parts and put new ones in. In fact, the components that make up the critical infrastructure are most probably not even manufactured anymore.

 DOI: 10.1201/9781003431633-4

Thus, new security layers must be added to what is already in place. But here lies another problem: one cannot simply add new security features; they also have to be interoperable with the components of the critical infrastructure, which is a very difficult feat to achieve. As a result, attacks on critical infrastructure will continue to happen, with much devastating consequences as time goes by.

In this chapter, we take a turn away from focusing exclusively from ransomware to now focusing on a tool that can greatly mitigate the risks of a ransomware attack from happening in the first place. This is known as "penetration testing," which will be further explored.

WHAT IS PENETRATION TESTING?

In its simplest terms, penetration testing can also be viewed as "ethical hacking". This is where an individual or even teams of individuals try to break down the walls of defenses of a business, in order to truly discover where both the known and unknown security vulnerabilities and gaps lie. Once these are discovered and documented, a report is then compiled for the client, detailing what has been found and what the recommendations are to remediate them. Typically, the penetration testing team does not implement these kinds of controls; rather, they are left to another entity known as the "managed service provider" (MSP) to deploy them.

A technical definition of penetration testing is as follows:

> A penetration test, also called a pen test or ethical hacking, is a cybersecurity technique that organizations use to identify, test and highlight vulnerabilities in their security posture. These penetration tests are often carried out by ethical hackers. These in-house employees or third parties mimic the strategies and actions of an attacker to evaluate the hackability of an organization's computer systems, network or web applications. Organizations can also use pen testing to evaluate their adherence to compliance regulations.
>
> Pen testing is considered a proactive cybersecurity measure because it involves consistent, self-initiated improvements based on the reports the test generates.
>
> (SOURCE: www.techtarget.com/searchsecurity/
> definition/penetration-testing)

Before we go deeper into penetration testing, here are some key facts to keep in mind:

- Conducting a penetration test has to be bound by a legal contract that is agreeable to both the client that is requesting the test and the organization that will be delivering it.

- The penetration test has to follow the letter of the law and any other forms of legal precedence that follow. This is to protect both parties, as previously reviewed. Anything that is to be done outside the bounds of the contract must first be approved in writing by the client.

- The client must be notified of every action that will be taken, and they not only have to agree to it, but they also have to approve it as well.

- As discussed, a report to the client must be provided by the penetration testing team. At a very high level, this must include all the tests that were carried out, what was discovered, all the vulnerabilities and weaknesses that were found, and all the remediations that should be followed to correct the weaknesses. Typically, this will involve the deployment of new controls. But in the end, it is entirely up to the client whether they wish to implement them or not, fully knowing the potential consequences if these recommended controls are not implemented.

- A penetration test can take some time if a proper and thorough one is to be conducted. Typically, it can last for a few days or even up to a few months.

- Conducting a penetration test typically involves multiple people being involved, and these are referred to as the Red Team, Blue Team, and Purple Team. Their exact functionalities will be explored and reviewed in this chapter.

- Penetration tests can be conducted either at the site of the client, or even remotely. But given the advances of technology today, most penetration tests are now conducted remotely.

- There are also automated tools that are available. For example, there are penetration testing software packages that are now available that can do all the tests on its own (primarily using both artificial intelligence and machine learning). There are also what are known as "autonomous" penetration testing software packages, which do not require human intervention. However, as it will be discussed at the end of the chapter, you need both to have a successful penetration test.

An example of a penetration test is illustrated next:

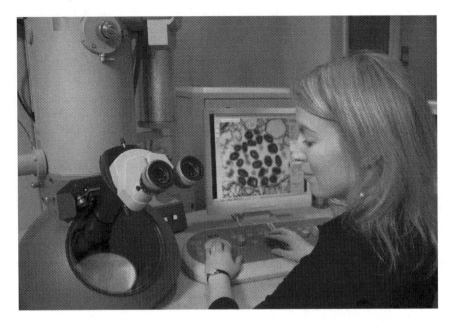

VULNERABILITY SCANNING AND PENETRATION TESTING

Before we fully explore in more detail what penetration testing is all about, it is important to note the differences between that and another testing mechanism called "vulnerability scanning". Although the two of them have the same objective in mind, their tests are completely different.

VULNERABILITY ASSESSMENTS

This type of test runs automated scans across the major components that reside in both your IT and network infrastructures. These primarily include the servers and other workstations and wireless devices. These assessments primarily look for known vulnerabilities that exist, without any human intervention involved.

A technical definition of a vulnerability scan is as follows:

> Vulnerability scanning is the process of identifying security weaknesses and flaws in systems and software running on them. This is an integral component of a vulnerability management program, which has one overarching goal – to protect the organization from breaches and the exposure of sensitive data. These programs rely on assessment to gauge security readiness and minimize risk, and vulnerability scanning is a critical tool in the cybersecurity toolbox.
>
> There are two big challenges related to traditional vulnerability assessment – knowing what to scan and knowing when to scan.
>
> (SOURCE: www.balbix.com/insights/
> what-is-vulnerability-scanning/)

The scans can run as short as a few minutes to as long as a few hours. After the probing has been completed, a report is usually generated for the client, and from there, it is up to them to decide how to proceed with any remediative actions.

This test is also "passive" kind of test in the sense that it only detects those weaknesses that are highly visible and can be exploited very easily by a cyberattacker. This just serves as a tipping point of what other vulnerabilities could be lurking. In a sense, the vulnerability scan can be viewed as merely conducting an EKG as to what is going on in terms of risk exposure.

One of the primary advantages of this kind of assessment is the cost. It is very affordable even to the SMB, which makes it a very attractive option. The downside is that if there are any recommendations that are provided in the report, it will not be specific to your business; rather, it will just be general in nature, based upon previous threat profiles. Because of its low cost, a vulnerability scan can be run on a continual cycle, at different timing intervals.

Further, the vulnerabilities that have been discovered are not exploited to see what the root causes are or if there are other vulnerabilities that could be lying underneath.

PENETRATION TESTING

This can be viewed as the "angiogram" in the detection of the vulnerabilities, weaknesses, and gaps that reside in your IT/network infrastructures.

A huge deep dive is done, with many kinds of tests being conducted. They won't last for just a matter of a few hours; rather, they go on for long and extended periods of time.

Second, there is not much automation that is involved when conducting a penetration test. It is primarily a manual process, which takes the work of many skilled professionals, with years of experience. These people are also known as "ethical hackers" because they take the mind-set of the cyberattacker and use every tactic in the book to break down your walls of defense.

With this effort, these individuals are not only looking for the known vulnerabilities, but they are also looking for the **unknown ones**, such as covert backdoors that could have been left behind in source code development. In other words, heavy active scanning is involved, unlike in vulnerability assessments.

Third, penetration testing is not just done on digital assets. It can also be used to unearth any gaps or weaknesses that are found within the physical infrastructure of a business. For example, a team can be specifically assigned to see how easy it is to replicate an ID badge and use that to fool the security guard at the main point of entry.

Fourth, penetration testing can be used to ascertain the level of vulnerability of the employees to a social engineering attack. In this regard, a specialized team can be called upon to make robocalls to the finance and accounting departments to see if they can be tricked into making payments on fake invoices. Or the calls could involve reaching out to the administrative assistants of the C-Suite and luring them to wire large sums of money to a phony, offshore account.

Fifth, penetration testing can be used in both the internal and external environments of a business.

Typically, there are at least two teams involved (perhaps even three) when conducting these kinds of tests, which are as follows:

- The Red Team: these are the ethical hackers that are trying to break into your systems as previously described;

- The Blue Team: these are the ethical hackers that work internally with your IT Security Team to determine how well they react to and fend off the attacks that are being launched toward them by the Red Team;

- The Purple Team: this may or may not be used, depending upon the security requirements of the client. This team is a combination of the

Red and Blue ones and provide an unbiased feedback to both teams as to how they have done during the course of the exercise.

At the end, the client is given an exhaustive report of the findings from the penetration test, as well as suggestions for remediative actions. Although the biggest advantage of this kind of exercise is the deep level of thoroughness that is involved, the downside is that they can be quite expensive. As a result, penetration tests are typically only carried out perhaps once, or at most, twice a year.

THE DIFFERENCES BETWEEN PENETRATION TESTING AND VULNERABILITY SCANNING – A MATRIX

The following matrix summarizes some of the key differences between a Vulnerability Scan and a penetration test:

Vulnerability Assessment	Penetration Test
Tests are passive	Tests are active
Tests are automated, no human intervention	Tests are primarily manual, lots of human intervention
Tests are short	Tests are much longer
Reports are provided to client but not specific to remediative actions	Reports are provided to client and are specific to remediative actions
Scans can be run on a continual cycle	Scanning is done only at point in time intervals due to their exhaustive nature
Tests are primarily done on digital assets	Tests are done on both physical and digital assets
Only known vulnerabilities are discovered	Both known and unknown vulnerabilities are discovered
Costs are affordable	Costs can be quite expensive
Only general tests are done	All kinds of tests are done, depending upon the requirements of the client

The question often gets asked: "What kind of test should I get"? It all comes down to cost. Typically, the smaller businesses can only afford the vulnerability scan, whereas the medium-sized business can afford the penetration test. But truthfully, every business should know all the vulnerabilities that lurk in their systems, especially the unknown ones, as this is what the cyberattacker will primarily go after.

A security breach can easily cost ten times more than any of these tests just described. Therefore, the CISO and his or her IT Security Team need to remain constantly proactive, thus making the penetration test the top choice to go with in the end. So, as one can see, penetration testing is deemed "active", and vulnerability scanning is deemed "passive".

THE TYPES OF PENETRATION TESTING

Although the kinds of tests and exercises to be performed will depend upon the exact needs of the client, typically, penetration testing falls under three distinct categories, which are as follows:

1) *White box testing*:

   This is where the penetration testing team has full and complete knowledge of the targets that they are going to study. Most likely, this will involve the components that reside from within the IT and network infrastructures of the client. This kind of testing is also technically known as "open glass, clear box, transparent or code-based testing".

2) *Black box testing*:

   This is where the penetration test team has no prior knowledge of the targets that are to be broken down. This is the most favored kind of penetration test, as the penetration testing team has to rely upon their own instincts and knowledge to carry out the tests. This is where the team members assume the true mind-set of a cyberattacker.

3) *Gray box testing*:

   This kind of penetration test is a combination of both white box testing and black box testing. Typically, this kind of testing procedure is used for examining the weaknesses found in source code, which are used to create and deploy web-based applications.

The latter test is described in more detail in the next subsection.

THE IMPORTANCE OF PENETRATION TESTING IN SOFTWARE DEVELOPMENT

It is important to keep in mind that software developers are very often under very serious time constraints to deliver the app on time and within budget, so testing for this kind of stuff is very often forgotten about. This is where the role of pen testing comes into play, and thus it is very important to partner up with a very well-established and reputable firm, such as CyberHunter Solutions, Inc.

Keep in mind that you should not wait until the very end of the development of the source code (especially just before it is expected to be released into production) to pen test it; rather, it should be done at different stages throughout the software development life cycle (SDLC). Here is why this is so important:

1) *To stay one step ahead of the automated hacking tools*:

   Given just about how everything is accessible on the Internet these days, there is a plethora of online hacking tools that are available online so that even the most amateur of hackers could break into the source code of your software application. Pen testing at different phases and continuing to do so even after the application has been released will ensure that it will not be vulnerable to all these hacking tools.

2) *Vulnerabilities can be fixed on time*:

   Let's face it, just about every product or service out there in the marketplace has some sort of security vulnerabilities and weaknesses in them, whether they are known or not. But by testing the source code ahead of time, you will be able to address them as they come up and fix them before moving onto the next step of the SDLC. This not only helps to ensure a much smoother transition to the production environment, but it will also help to deliver the project on time to the customer. For example, if you wait until the very last minute to Pen test the source code, and if a lot of vulnerabilities are found that need to be fixed, this will definitely push the delivery date by quite a bit, thus incurring extra expenses not only for the software development team, but for the customer as well.

3) *The detection of security vulnerabilities that may have already existed*:

   In the previous examples, we have examined the importance of pen testing at the different stages of the SDLC. What happens if you depend on a third party to develop the source code you need, and they claim that they have tested it in terms of security and that all is "up to snuff"? Do you take faith in their word, and go ahead and deploy the application? Well, this is a situation that you never want to be in. If you are in this scenario, it is your responsibility to make sure that the source code is tested thoroughly for any security gaps and weaknesses that may have already existed and that they are remediated before the actual application is launched. It is also quite important that you keep pen testing this source code (as well as for other software applications that you may have) regularly, so that any future vulnerabilities can be detected and patched up quickly. By doing this, you are not only enforcing a proactive mind-set with your IT Security Team, but you are also instilling a sense of a high level of confidence in your customers that you take protecting their personal identifiable information (PII) very seriously.

4) *To help prepare for the worst-case scenario*:

Just suppose that after all this pen testing that you have done, the software application in question has been hit by a cyberattacker (as previously mentioned, there is no guarantee in anything). Well, all is not completely lost. By having done so many of these exercises, your IT Security Team will be able to respond to that threat and mitigate much quicker than if they have never practiced it before. The result is a much-reduced downtime, and you will be able to bring back your mission-critical business processes much more quickly.

5) *It will allow you to stay ahead in terms of compliance*:

Given the ever-changing dynamics of the cyber threat landscape, pretty much all businesses are coming under the scrutiny of government auditors to make sure that any customer data that they gather and retain comes into compliance with such regulations as HIPAA, GDPR, the ISO 27001, PCI Data Security Standards, etc. If an organization fails in any regard, stiff fines and penalties can be imposed. Conducting regular pen testing on the source code as it is the various SDLC phases and after shows the auditors you are taking these various regulations very seriously and that protection of customer information/data is of paramount importance.

THE STEPS IN PENETRATION TESTING

Before a penetration testing team can conduct any kind or type of test, it is essential that they first lay out the proverbial "plan of attack". This is done to get the big picture of what is to be done, how it will be carried out, and what the results could look like. Here are the steps in this process, at a macro level:

1) *The reconnaissance phase*:

   This is where the penetration testing team studies everything they can about the targets to be broken down. Any relevant information and data are taken from the following sources:

   - Searching the Internet;

   - Domain name information and data;

   - Dumpster diving;

   - Network scanning.

   Another method that is used here is "social engineering". This is where the cyberattacker cons the employee of a company into giving out confidential information and data about their business by preying upon certain human vulnerabilities. A technical definition of it is as follows:

Social engineering is the art of manipulating people so they give up confidential information. The types of information these criminals are seeking can vary, but when individuals are targeted the criminals are usually trying to trick you into giving them your passwords or bank information, or access your computer to secretly install malicious software–that will give them access to your passwords and bank information as well as giving them control over your computer.

Criminals use social engineering tactics because it is usually easier to exploit your natural inclination to trust than it is to discover ways to hack your software. For example, it is much easier to fool someone into giving you their password than it is for you to try hacking their password (unless the password is really weak).

(SOURCE: www.webroot.com/us/en/resources/
tips-articles/what-is-social-engineering)

An example of social engineering is illustrated next:

2) *Scanning*:

This is where the penetration testing team launches all its methods to find all the weaknesses, vulnerabilities, and gaps in targets that have been identified and agreed to by the client and the penetration testing organization. Typically, this will include artifacts in the cloud through a deployment (such as the AWS or Azure), servers (both physical and virtual), e-mail systems, domain names, and the source code of any web-based application. But also keep in mind that penetration testing does not have to involve just digital assets. It can also include physical assets. For example, a penetration testing team could even be called out to launch mock social engineering exercises against the employees of a company (as just discussed).

3) *Gaining the access*:

Once everything is known in the last step, the penetration testing team will then try to infiltrate the systems, as just described. Given the cyberattacks of today, the goal here is to see how long they can stay inside the target, without being noticed. A typical test here would be that of data exfiltration, where the PII datasets of both employees and customers (as reviewed earlier in this book) are heisted, in a covert fashion, once again, not to the knowledge of the unsuspecting victim.

4) *Staying Inside*:

Once the penetration testing team has gained a foothold on the inside, the goal in this last step is to see what kinds and types of malicious payloads they can deploy, once again, being unnoticed. For example, SQL injection payloads, Trojan Horses, worms, viruses, key logging software, and other types of malware could be deployed. It is important to keep in mind that in this particular phase, any malicious payloads that are deployed will be highly controlled by the penetration testing team, so that no actual damage can be caused.

These steps are illustrated in the following diagram:

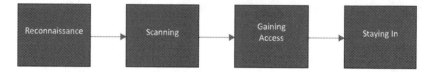

THE TYPES OF TARGETS IN PENETRATION TESTING

Although we have highlighted the targets that can be used by a penetration testing team, it is important to provide a more detailed explanation. The specific targets are as follows:

1) *The web apps*:

This target is probably the most widely studied by a penetration testing team. The reason for this is that web-based applications are now the predominant type of service that is most in demand today by customers, especially when it comes to creating an e-commerce store. As previously mentioned, testing the security of the source code in these applications is often a last priority for software developers, but now there is a rising trend where penetration testing of the source code is being requested. Also, application programming interfaces (APIs) are now being tested, as many of them are open source and have not been upgraded or deployed with the most recent software patches and upgrades.

2) *The mobile apps*:

Just like the web-based apps, mobile apps are also starting to receive penetration tests. This is not only being asked more by the client for whom the app is being developed, but also by Google and Apple, as they are now becoming much more stringent in terms of the mobile apps that they allow to be uploaded onto their respective stores. In this regard, both the server side (the back end) and the client side (the front end) are being fully tested.

3) *The network*:

This continues to be an item that is constantly being penetration tested primarily because private and confidential data is being transmitted daily. Examples of items that are tested are the transport protocols and the SSL certificates.

4) *The cloud*:

Typically, penetration testing has been associated with an on premises infrastructure. But with most of the businesses now making a full migration to the cloud (either the AWS or Azure), penetration testing is now being used to find the weaknesses and vulnerabilities in virtual machines, virtual desktops, virtual databases, etc. In fact, the same techniques that are used for penetration testing an on premises IT/network infrastructure is also used for a cloud-based deployment, whether it is a private cloud, public cloud, or even a hybrid cloud.

5) *The cloud container*:

This is a cloud-based service, offered mostly by the AWS and Azure. This is where a single software application can be stored and tested for later deployments into the production environment. The container is called a "Docker".

6) *Wireless devices*:

With the nearly 99% remote workforce today in corporate America, mobile devices have become a prime target for the cyberattacker. primarily because employees now conduct their daily job tasks on their smartphone. Examples of penetration testing sub-targets in this include the following:

- Authentication and/or authorization mechanisms;

- Security controls as they relate to two-factor authentication or multifactor authentication (2FA and MFA, respectively);

- Other kinds of server-side issues.

THE PENETRATION TESTING TEAMS

So far in this chapter, we have talked about the penetration testing team. But what and who are they? We take a closer look at them in these next three subsections.

The Red Team

It is the Red Team that has the primary responsibility of launching an "ethically based" cyberattack against the defense perimeters of your business. But it is important to note here that the Red Team is not particularly interested in what is being attacked, *they are much more interested instead in the access methods to get to those targets*.

The Red Team will use a large amount of creativity and even use techniques one may never even have heard of. Remember, the goal of the Red Team is to not just attack your lines of defense but breach them through every means that are available at their disposal. To do this, they will think and act just like the real cyberattacker but very often come up with ideas on their own as well.

When a Red Team engages in its mock cyberattacks, they very often do not ask for a specific list of targets to hit. Rather, they are also interested in those systems in your IT Infrastructure that are "out of scope" as well. As a result, this gives the Red Team a much broader set of permutations to examine. Because of this, the Red Team will "find vulnerabilities that stem from cultural bias in system design, flawed conclusions, or the limitations and expectations of an insider perspective" (Source: www.senseofsecurity. com.au/consulting/red-team-testing/).

It is important to note that Red Teams often use a methodology known as the "layered approach". With this, multiple attempts are utilized to break through the lines of defense at the business entity. These attempts are not made successively; rather, they are done simultaneously to cause the highest levels of confusion and mayhem for the Blue Team.

For example, one part of the Red Team may try to hack into the password database, while at the same time, another part of the Red Team could try to gain access to the main entry of the organization by using covertly replicated access cards.

It is important to note that effective Red Team Testing just does not happen over a short period of time. It can take up to a year to examine what to hit, as a real cyberattacker these days will take their own time as well in determining and researching their targets.

A primary advantage of having a Red Team conduct your penetration testing is that they will offer an unbiased, holistic view of the weaknesses not only in your IT Infrastructure, but also among your employees and the physical conditions of your office location(s).

The Blue Team

The overarching task of the Blue Team is fight off the cyberattack that has been launched by the Red Team. They will also work in conjunction with your existing IT Security Team in this regard. But apart from this, the Blue Team has other specific responsibilities in the efforts to overcome the cyberattack. These are as follows:

1) Preparedness:

The Blue Team will do everything possible in its role to protect the business or corporation from any looming cyber-based threats. This will include testing all the Security technologies that are in place to make sure that they are optimized to detect any sort of anomalies or outliers; making sure that the incident response and the disaster recovery plans are set in motion should a cyberattack actually occur; and *keeping all employees informed* of the upcoming cyber threat landscape.

2) Identification:

Here, the Blue Team will make every effort to correctly identify any potential cyberattacks that are posed to the business or corporation.

3) Containment:

If the organization is hit by a cyberattack, it will then become the responsibility of the Blue Team to contain the damage caused by the attack. In this regard, one of the best tools that the Blue Team will have at hand is the Incident Response Plan. By initiating it at the time of the cyberattack, the members of the Incident Response Team will also be called into action to mitigate any losses from the cyberattack.

4) Recovery:

In the unfortunate chance that the business or corporation gets breached by a cyberattack, it will also be one of the main responsibilities of the Blue Team to activate the disaster recovery plans in order to bring the entity back at a predefined level of operations before the incident occurred. This should occur, at a maximum, no more than one or two days after the cyberattack. At this point, one of the main priorities of the Blue Team is to bring up as many mission-critical processes as possible during this short time span.

5) Lessons learned:

Obviously, once the damage from the cyberattack has been mitigated, and the organization is up and running at nearly 100% operational levels, a Forensics Investigation Team will be called in to conduct an exhaustive study on what happened and how the cyberattack could have been avoided. It is also one of the responsibilities of the Blue Team to compile all of this into a report, as well as to formulate strategies on how such types of incidents can be avoided in the future.

During the penetration testing exercise(s), the Blue Team also assumes the following responsibilities:

1) Operation system hardening:

The Blue Team will further fortify the operating systems of all the hardware that is being used at the business or corporation. This will include primarily all the servers, workstations, and wireless devices (securing both the Android and iOS). The goal here is to decrease the "surface of vulnerability" of all the operating systems that are currently being used.

2) The perimeter defense:

The Blue Team will also ensure that all firewalls, network intrusion devices, routers, traffic flow devices, packet filtering devices, etc. are all up and running and operating at peak conditions.

To further fend off any cyberattacks, the Blue Team typically uses tools such as log management and analysis, and security information and event management (SIEM) technology.

The Purple Team

The primary objective of the Purple Team is to maximize the capabilities of both the Red Team and the Blue Team. For example, with the former, the Purple Team can "evaluate your security controls and ability to detect attacks, compromise, lateral movement, command and control communications, and data exfiltration".

In other words, after the Red Team has evaluated what kind of cyberattacks they are going to launch toward your lines of defense, the Purple Team can also further enhance these efforts by brainstorming newer kinds of cyber threats that can be launched, as well as new attack vectors.

In turn, the Purple Team can also work hand in hand with the Blue Team to make sure that they have followed the steps for cyberattack preparedness. In this regard, the Purple Team can also conduct a comprehensive audit check to ensure that the Blue Team has not left anything out in their preparation processes.

This scenario is illustrated in the following diagram:

In fact, the Purple Team should be viewed as a "neutral party" when a penetration testing exercise(s) is being carried out. In other words, they do not merely attack or defend, they actually do both, and also lend a hand to both sides of the equation by sharing intelligence. Different members of the Red Team and the Blue Team will take their own corresponding turns on participating in the Purple Team. In this regard, the size of the Purple Team should be kept relatively small – perhaps no more than two members from either the Red Team or the Blue Team. But in the end, it is not the size of the team that matters, it is the level and the breadth of the team member's experience that matters the most.

Some of the primary objectives of a Purple Team include the following:

1) *Working harmoniously with both the Red Team and the Blue Team*:

This includes making observations and notes on how the two teams are working together, making any recommendations to change the team compositions, or making any needed adjustments to the penetration exercise(s) themselves.

2) *Understanding and visualizing the big picture*:

This means assuming the frame of mind, thinking processes, and the responsibilities of both the Red Team and the Blue Team.

3) *Assuming an overall responsibility for the penetration testing exercise(s)*:

This simply refers to analyzing and interpreting results for the client and taking remedial or corrective actions that are needed. For example, this could include coming up with a schedule for downloading and implementing software patches and upgrades and providing recommendations to improve security awareness training for the employees of the organization that is being penetration tested.

4) *Delivering the maximum value to the client*:

By collecting information and data from both the Red Team and the Blue Team, the Purple Team can, as stated before, deliver a high-quality document to the client, with the result being that the lines of defenses will only be that much more fortified.

A DEEPER DIVE INTO WEB APPLICATION PENETRATION TESTING

In this chapter, we have alluded quite heavily to the importance of penetration testing for web-based applications. In this subsection, we provide some intricacies that are involved with it.

In today's digital world, everything is pretty much made available by the Internet. Because of this, the demand for robust and effective web-based applications remains strong and will continue to be so for a very long time. A major catalyst for this has been the advent of the remote workforce, with just about all employees using web interfaces to get their daily job tasks done.

Thus, the need to critically test web applications before they are deployed into the production environment is now greater than ever before. This is where the role of penetration testing comes into play. Put in simple terms, the goal of conducting these kinds of exercises is to see where all the vulnerabilities, weaknesses, and gaps reside in them. Once all of these have been assessed, remediative actions are then provided so that they will not be an issue once the actual product has been sent to the client.

This kind of testing is normally quite exhaustive in nature and typically involves checking for the following:

- Overall functionality;
- Built-in functionality;
- Databases.

The next subsection provides a more detailed overview of these.

The Components of Web App Penetration Testing

Although the depth and the scope of the exact penetration test (aka "pen test") to be executed is primarily dependent upon the needs of the client, to varying degrees, they typically include the following:

1) *The testing for overall functionality*:

This involves testing for different items such as the graphical user interface (GUI) interface, the APIs that are being used (especially if they are open sourced in nature); the databases that will be populated with confidential information and data, which include the personal identifiable information (PII) datasets; and other financial data that will be stored in them by the customer as well as testing the web application from both the server side (which involves testing the server upon which the web application is hosted) and the client side (this is the interface that the end user will interact with on a day-to-day basis).

2) *The testing for built-in functionality*:

This kind of examination usually looks at seeing how the individual components of the web application work together in a holistic fashion, and the following is usually tested the most:

- The testing of all links. This includes the outbound links, internal links, any "mail to" links, and anchor links.

- The checking of forms. This mostly involves the "Contact Us" page, but it can include others as well, such as the ones used for lead generation purposes. In this regard, all the scripts must be checked (for example, most of these are written in PHP, Perl, etc.); any default fields must be populated with the correct numerical values; confirming that the right information/data that is entered in by the end user is being transmitted and stored into the database(s); making sure that the UI/UX environment is compatible with all platforms (such as the Android and the iOS) and all devices (like notebooks, tablets, smartphones, etc.). Also, given the ramifications of both the general data protection regulation (GDPR) and the California Consumer Privacy Act (CCPA), you also need to make sure that the appropriate verbiage exists on the web application, stating that the end user agrees to have their information stored, and if not, how they can opt out of it.

- The testing of cookies. This procedure involves making sure that they are appropriately deleted or expire when they are supposed to.

- The testing of both the hyper text markup language (HTML) and the cascading style sheets (CSS). This is probably one of the most critical aspects. Although other different web application programming languages can be used in lieu of the HTML, the bottom line is that the code used to create the web application must be tested inside and out, especially when it comes to the usage of APIs. If this is not done, there are backdoors that can be left behind, thus leaving a gaping point of entry for the cyberattacker.

- The examination of compliance requirements. With data privacy now becoming quite a hot-button topic, you also need to pen test the source code so that is not only compliant with the GDPR and the CCPA, but also with the various National Institute of Science and Technology (NIST) and International Organization for Standardization (ISO) standards and those that have been set forth by the W3C.

3) *The testing of the database functionality*:

Although this kind of test was addressed in overall functionality, it is still extremely important to test the database(s) that will be connected to the web application. Whatever tool is used to create them (such as SQL Server, MySQL, etc.), the following must be examined:

- The examination of any errors that may come up as result of executing any type or kind of query. This can be accomplished by using test data sets.

- Confirming that any data or information that is transmitted to and from the end user and web application remains intact and stays that way after it is stored in the database. Equally important here is ensuring that the layers of encryption that have been deployed are strong enough and are difficult to break through.

- Making sure that the response to any queries is handled in an optimal way and is done within a well-established time limit. It is important to keep in mind that if the response time is too long, this can "hang up" the web application and could pose a serious security vulnerability.

DISTINGUISHING THE EXTERNAL PENETRATION TEST

It is important to note that penetration testing can take place from within the confines of the IT and network infrastructure of a business as well as the external environment. It is with the latter environment that most penetration testing is being used, so therefore, it is important to examine it at a deeper level.

What Is It?

When people talk about penetration testing, they often confuse the internal kind with the external one. However, there are key differences between the two. For example, with the former, the pen testing team is looking for vulnerabilities that may lie from within the internal environment of your business. This typically includes the following:

- Access points (these can include both logical- and physical-based);
- The Wi-Fi system;
- Firewalls, routers, and network intrusion devices.

But with the latter, the following are examined to ascertain the weaknesses that could exist from the outside environment of your business. In other words, you want to find out where those undiscovered gaps are if a cyberattacker were to attack your lines of defense from the outside going in (after all, that is their primary objective in the end).

The testing here typically includes the following:

- Source code testing (especially those of web-based applications);
- Identity management testing;
- Authentication/authorization testing;

- The testing of any other types of client-facing applications (this is now becoming very crucial, especially as the remote workforce now starts to take a permanent hold);

- The testing of the integrity of the lines of network communications, especially taking a very careful examination of the virtual private networks (VPNs) that are currently being used;

- The testing of the various session management systems that are taking place between the server and the client, as you do not want network-based requests to go unfulfilled for an extensive period of time;

- The testing and examination of any encryption-based systems that are deployed along your lines of defense.

The Stages of External Penetration Testing

It is important to keep in mind that conducting this kind of test simply does not just involve putting a Red Team (these are the ethical hackers that try to penetrate your business from the external environment) and simply throwing everything that they have at their disposal against your digital assets. Rather, a methodological approach needs to be taken, and the following are the major components of it:

1) *The planning and reconnaissance phase*:

Shortly after all the contracts and legal agreements have been signed between the company doing the actual pen test and the client, this is the first step that needs to be accomplished. With this, the Red Team will take time and prioritize what needs to be done first. For example, they will attempt to gain a comprehensive understanding of those types of threat variants that your business is most prone to by carefully studying the risk assessment analysis that you initially conducted. From here, the Red Team can target the most vulnerable digital assets first. Apart from this, they can also conduct various online testing exercises to pinpoint other facets that need to be examined as well, such as those items that did not appear in the analysis. This phase can be deemed to be the information gathering session, so that the Red Team can get a detailed, holistic view of what your entire IT and network infrastructure looks like.

2) *The Scanning of the targets*:

This is the stage where the Red Team will take the mind-set of a real-world cyberattacker with a nefarious intent and start to hit upon those targets that appear to offer the most prized possessions that can be yielded. This includes items such as confidential company documents, intellectual property (IP), the personal identifiable information (PII) datasets of both your customers and employees (typically this will be credit card numbers, Social Security numbers, usernames/passwords, and other sorts of banking/financial information), etc. Some examples of the targets in this aspect include the following:

- Servers that contain shared resources;
- Databases that house the mission critical information/data;
- The identification of any shared or open parts that exist in your network infrastructure;
- The location of FTP servers (because usernames and passwords are usually entered in as cleartext here);
- Any E-mail servers;
- The location of any outdated or weak SSL certificates in an effort to deploy malicious payloads that can be used, for example, in a SQL injection attack.

3) *The gaining and maintaining of access*:

Once the weak spots have been determined from the second step, the next phase is to attempt to gain access to them and maintain access for as long as possible. This is usually done by finding and locating those backdoors that were not known before. It is important to keep in mind that the cyberattacker is not going to just find one way in. They will try to find all possible avenues, so they can use a combination of them at infrequent intervals to go undiscovered.

4) *The exploitation*:

Once the Red Team has gained access to what they have laid down the objectives for, the final step in the exercise is to now try to further exploit all the weaknesses, gaps, and vulnerabilities that have been discovered and steal the proverbial "Crown Jewels". One thing that should be noted here is that the Red Team will try to stay as long as possible in whatever they have penetrated and to launch the exfiltration process slowly, bit by bit at a time. The goal of this is to avoid the detection by the internal network systems by not giving out any kind of abnormal behavioral signatures, which can happen if the "Crown Jewels" were being taken out in bigger chunks.

THE TYPES OF PENETRATION TESTING TOOLS

So far in this chapter, we have covered the following concepts as they relate to penetration testing:

- What Is Penetration Testing?

- Vulnerability Scanning and Penetration Testing

- The Differences between Penetration Testing and Vulnerability Scanning – a Matrix

- The Types of Penetration Testing

- The Importance of Penetration Testing in Software Development

- The Steps in Penetration Testing

- The Types of Targets in Penetration Testing

- The Penetration Testing Teams

- A Deeper Dive into Web Application Penetration Testing

- Distinguishing the External Penetration Test

Now at this point, it is important to get an idea of some of the examples of software-based tools that the penetration testing teams use when they conduct their specific exercises. A survey of these tools is shown in the following matrix:

Penetration Testing Tool	Distinguishing Characteristics
Kali Linux	• This is by far the most widely used penetration technology today.
	• It is typically deployed on a virtual machine (VM).
	• It is only used for offensive testing, not defensive testing, thus making it very exploitable.
Nmap	• This is an acronym that stands for "network mapping".
	• It is used to detect open ports on a network and discover their weaknesses and vulnerabilities.
	• It is typically used to scan the entire range of the IPv4 TCIP/IP address range.
Metasploit	• The mantra for this tool is: "Aim at your target, pick your exploit, select a payload, and fire".
	(Source: www.csoonline.com/article/2943524/11-penetration-testing-tools-the-pros-use.html)
	• It also automates the processes for a penetration test.
Wireshark	• This tool analyzes all types and kinds of network protocols.
	• All analysis is done in real time.
John the Ripper	• This is a password cracker, designed to break passwords.
	• It is used both online and offline.
Hashcat	• It is used to break hashing algorithms.
	• It can be used to launch dictionary attacks.
	• It is also widely used to guess passwords of all kinds and types.
Hydra	• This is used to crack SSH, FTP, IMAP, IRC, RDP, and other kinds of network connection protocols.
Burp Suite	• This is deemed one of the most expensive penetration testing tools, at $3,999 per year.
	• It is used primarily to detect vulnerabilities in web-based applications.
Zed Attack Proxy	• This allows you to examine the network traffic between your web browser and the website that you are visiting.
sqlmap	• This tool examines the vulnerabilities that exist in all kinds of SQL-based databases, such as MySQL, ProstGRESSQL, and SL Server.
	• It can also work with Oracle and Microsoft Access.
	• It is primarily used to test for SQL injection attacks.
Aircrack-ng	• This is a tool that is primarily used to test the vulnerabilities in home-based networks.

THE CATEGORIES OF PENETRATION TESTING TOOLS

All the previously mentioned penetration testing falls into these specific categories, which are examined in the following matrix:

Category	Characteristics
Network Penetration Testing	• These are used to test the weaknesses in all sorts of network connections, especially TCP/IP.
Web Application Testing	• These are used to test the back end and front of all web applications.
Database Testing	• These are used to ascertain the weaknesses of all databases, whether they are closed source or open source.
Automated Penetration Testing	• These are tools that use a combination of AI and ML to automate the mundane and routine processes of a penetration test.
Open Source Testing	• These tools use the open source model and are free to use.

(*Source:* www.csoonline.com/article/2943524/11-penetration-testing-tools-the-pros-use. html)

THE NEXT GENERATION OF PENETRATION TESTING – THE "AS A SERVICE" MODEL

As was mentioned earlier in this chapter, penetration testing tools can be fully automated or fully autonomous. Or perhaps, it could even be a combination of both of them. This is where a penetration testing tool can run on its own, without needing human intervention, at least theoretically. But now, there is a new type of penetration testing model that is coming out, and this is known as "Penetration testing as a Service". The basic crux of this is that it follows the same kind of "as a Service" deployment models that you typically see with the cloud. But there are some notable differences, which include the following:

- The end user can pick both automated and human intervention penetration testing services.

- Unlike the traditional "as a Service" models, the pricing is not fixed on a monthly basis, and thus can drastically change from month to month.

- Unlike the SaaS (Software as a Service) model, the Penetration testing as a Service model may not fit all the environments. For example, if you have a complex testing environment, you are probably better off hiring an actual penetration testing organization.

- Unlike a SaaS model, the Penetration testing as a Service model does not allow for custom configuration. While you can pick those tools you want, those will have to be customized on a case-by-case basis.

But there are also distinct advantages, which include the following:

1) You have freedom to choose the kinds and types of penetration testing services that you want.

2) You can hire a penetration testing team in less than 24 hours.

3) You can have 24 x 7 x 365 monitoring by selecting the automated services you need.

4) You can keep doing penetration tests at a very affordable price (by comparison, a one-time penetration test can run as much as $30,000–$40,000).

5) You can get access to all reports within minutes after a test is conducted and even get access to all the information and data that was used.

6) It can easily integrate with any DevOps or even DevSecOps tools.

In the end, penetration testing is probably the best and only way to truly determine what the weaknesses, gaps, and vulnerabilities are in your IT and network infrastructures, in order to mitigate the risks of a ransomware attack from happening to your business. But keep in mind, it takes the best of both worlds to make all these happen: Technology + Human Intervention. You cannot go to the extreme in either direction to get the best results and controls to be deployed.

CHAPTER 4

How to Recover from a Ransomware Attack

S O FAR IN THIS book, we have provided an in-depth review of what ransomware is, reviewed some of the more famous ransomware attacks, and provided details on how penetration testing is probably best the weapon out there for combatting a ransomware attack. But now the last piece of the puzzle still exists – what does a business do after it has been impacted by a ransomware attack? Well, there two keys to the puzzle here:

- Containing the ransomware attack on a real-time basis;

- Recovering from any damage or impacts that it may have caused.

The best way to practice these two is to have an "incident response plan" and a "disaster recovery plan". In this chapter, we look at the components that should be included in both. But keep in mind that you cannot simply write a comprehensive plan just based on this chapter. A lot of what should be contained will depend, of course, on the digital assets that are in your IT and network infrastructure, and what your own security requirements and needs are at the time of document evolution.

This chapter just gives you a framework of what you should consider implementing. So first, let us start with the incident response plan.

DOI: 10.1201/9781003431633-5

THE COMPONENTS OF AN INCIDENCE RESPONSE PLAN

As its name implies, an incident response plan (IR plan) details the steps and actions that your company needs to take to contain a security breach, such as a ransomware attack. The technical definition for an IR plan is as follows:

> An Incident Response Plan is a written document, formally approved by the senior leadership team, that helps your organization before, during, and after a confirmed or suspected security incident. Your IRP will clarify roles and responsibilities and will provide guidance on key activities. It should also include a cybersecurity list of key people who may be needed during a crisis.
>
> (SOURCE: www.cisa.gov/sites/default/files/publications/ Incident-Response-Plan-Basics_508c.pdf).

An example of an incident response is illustrated next:

The Overall Flow of an Incident Response

It is important to note that in responding to an incident, such as a ransomware attack, exact procedures must be followed so that no extra time is wasted, where it matters the most. The overall Incident Response should follow something like this:

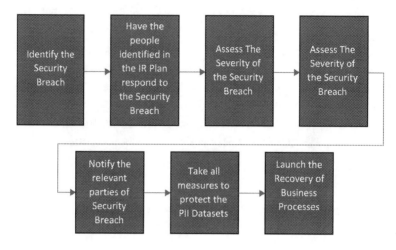

The Components of an Incident Response Plan

The following are the items that you should consider putting into your respective IR plan:

1) *Identify who will be specifically involved with the incidence response communications team*:

   In this component of the plan, it is very crucial that the right people from all the departments of the business or corporation are selected. Once selected, these individuals must then understand the gravity of their responsibilities, as they must be able to respond quickly at a moment without hesitation. The key individuals who need to be included on this team include the following:

   • The CEO, CFO, and the CIO or CISO;

   • A representative from the public relations department;

   • A representative from the investor relations department;

   • A representative from the human resources department;

   • A representative from the sales and marketing department.

   It is also important that at least two individuals from these respective departments should be trained in how to handle any communications or queries from the media. An alternate to each representative should also be picked in case the primary representative cannot be reached during the time of crisis.

2) *Have mechanisms in place by which employees can help communicate any unforeseen threats*:

In this regard, there should be an open line of communications in which feedback from employees is solicited across all departments of the organization, and at all levels. The goal here is to have the ability to report any new threats and even new ideas for the continuous refinement of the incident response communications process to the appropriate representative of the IR Communications Team (as just described). By having this line of communications in place, a proactive security mind-set will thus be instilled among all employees of the business or corporation.

3) *Create and develop the messaging around the risks that have been identified*:

After the representatives have been selected and the open lines of communications established, the next step is to create the messaging for each kind of cyber risk to which the organization is prone. Obviously, the details of what will be communicated to the public and other key stakeholders will vary if an organization is actually hit by a cyberattack. But at this point in the incident response communications plan, it is important to have at least the messaging template prepared so that the designated representatives of the various departments will be able to communicate with confidence and effectiveness.

4) *Create the internal contact roster*:

This component of the incident response communications plan is one of the most important. After all, once a business or corporation is hit by a cyberattack, the first thing that will come to mind is contacting the department representatives to determine exactly what is happening and the degree of damage. In this regard, it becomes critical to have all the contact information (which includes work E-Mail, personal E-Mail, work cell number, personal cell number, and even home telephone number) for each of the department representatives. All this contact information should be documented in an easy and quick-to-read format, such as a call tree. Also, it is important to include all this contact information for the alternate department representative. The bottom line here is that all the contact information must be up to date and confirmed at least once a month for any changes.

5) *Identify and establish relationships with the key stakeholders of the organization*:

Apart from communicating with employees and the department representatives, it is also equally important to reach out to the stakeholders that have a vested interest in the well-being of the organization at the time of crisis. Such individuals include the following:

- Investors and shareholders;

- Customers and business partners;

- Suppliers and distributors;

- Any relevant government official at the local level.

This component of the incident response communications plan is often overlooked; therefore, it is important to include all their contact information in the call tree as well. The call tree should be made available to all department representatives (including their alternates) and key stakeholders in printed, electronic, and online formats.

Finally, it is important for a business or a corporation to not only focus on preparing for just one type or kind of cyberattack but also take a holistic view, which will thus allow you to prepare for any cyberattack.

The Communications Process

As one can see, communications is of utmost importance in any kind or type of incident response. If there is not a proper line of communications that has been established, precious time will be wasted that can be used to combat the actual ransomware attack:

The following matrix identifies the titles and roles of the members of the Incident Response Team:

Title	Role
Team Leader	Responsible for the overall incident response; will coordinate the necessary actions.
Incident Lead	Responsible for coordinating the actual response.
IT Contact	Responsible for communications between the incident lead and other members of the IT staff.
Legal Representative	Responsible for leading the legal aspects of the incident response.
Public Relations Officer	Responsible for protecting and promoting the image of the business entity during an incident response.
Management Team	Responsible for approving and directing security policy during an incident response.

The Benefits of a Quick Response

As mentioned earlier, responding quickly to a ransomware attack is of paramount importance. There are certain benefits to be gained, which are as follows:

1) *The downtime, if any, will be minimized*:

   The business or the corporation will be able to come back to full operations quickly, assuming that there is a proper incident response plan put into place and that all sensitive data has been backed up properly and can be accessed efficiently and quickly. The result is that, depending upon the severity of the cyberattack, the financial bottom line of the company should not be too greatly impacted. Also, responding quickly to an incident will mean that any vulnerabilities that have been exploited by the cyberattacker will be minimized, and it will also reduce the risk of the same incident happening to a different part of the organization.

2) *Immediately notifying your customers as to what happened could in the long run win new business*:

   For example, when you communicate with your customer in a timely manner, it shows them that not only do you take your due diligence seriously but that you also care about them on a much more personal level. In fact, many organizations fail because many customers do not know they too have become a victim until much later. In these instances, very often a letter is mailed out, thus leaving an "impersonal effect". So, the manner and the time frame in which a customer is contacted can make a huge difference. A phone call to the customer from a member of the management team shortly after an incident has taken place would leave a much more "personalized effect"; it will prove to them that by taking the time and effort to use this mode of communication, you take their security very seriously. Thus, in the end, this personal touch will create a much more favorable and long-lasting impression on the customer, which could bring in more repeat as well as referable business later.

3) *Responding in a timely manner to any kind of security breach will allow for a thorough investigation*:

This will mean that the evidence will still be fresh and intact, thus allowing for any forensic information and data to be collected quickly. This, of course, translates into evidence that will be admissible in a court of law and that can also be used to bring the cyberattacker to justice.

THE COMPONENTS OF A DISASTER RECOVERY PLAN

Once your business has reacted promptly and mitigated the further spread of the ransomware attack through the use of the incident response plan, the next step is bringing back up the mission critical processes of your business. It is important to keep in mind that the time for all of this to happen will not only depend upon how big your business is, but also on how much damage has been done.

You should not attempt to recover everything in one fell swoop, but rather, your first priority is to bring up your mission critical processes first, which serves the needs of both your employees and customers. Typically, there is confusion between the incident response plan and the disaster recovery plan, but the two are quite different from each other. For example, the technical definition of a disaster recovery plan is as follows:

A disaster recovery plan (DRP) is a documented, structured approach that describes how an organization can quickly resume work after an unplanned incident. A DRP is an essential part of a business continuity plan (BCP). It is applied to the aspects of an organization that depend on a functioning information technology (IT) infrastructure. A DRP aims to help an organization resolve data loss and recover system functionality so that it can perform in the aftermath of an incident, even if it operates at a minimal level.

(SOURCE: www.techtarget.com/searchdisasterrecovery/definition/disaster-recovery-plan)

An illustration of a disaster recovery is as follows:

But just like the incident response plan, keep in mind that the next items are to be considered part of the overall disaster recovery plan. How it will be ultimately crafted will depend primarily upon your security requirements.

1) *Create the disaster recovery team*:

This is probably one of the most crucial aspects of the disaster recovery plan. This will be the team of your employees that will be responsible for acting on their own areas to bring the business back up and running as quickly as possible after you have been hit by a cyberattack. This area should clearly detail the following:

- The team members who will be part of the actual Disaster Recovery Team;

- Their specific responsibilities;

- Most importantly, their contact information. This should include work phone number, work E-mail address, home phone number, and personal E-mail address as well. Also, make sure to include all cell phone numbers, both work and personal.

It is important to note that the team members should include representatives from all the departments that you may have. Depending upon how large the business is, upper management and even the C-Suite should also be included. Remember, clear and concise communications among all the team members here is crucial, as any time wasted will only translate into further downtime, which could be detrimental in the end. Also, make sure that all contact information is up to date as well.

2) *Moving your equipment*:

Depending upon the kind of disaster recovery setup you choose to establish (as reviewed in the last section), the disaster recovery plan needs to have a component as to how all the employee-related equipment will be moved. Although your IT Infrastructure will be replicated in a cloud Infrastructure or at the secondary physical site, there are still things that must be immediately transitioned over, for your employees to bring your business back up to a normal state of operations once again. This includes all workstations, computers, and wireless devices that are used to conduct everyday job functions. In this regard, it is also wise to make advanced plans with a moving company that specializes in disaster recovery so that items can be moved very quickly. Your Disaster Recovery Team should also keep an active inventory of all these items, and make sure that it is always updated.

3) *Daily checks on the data backups*:

Although the backup databases and the confidential information and data they contain will either reside in a cloud infrastructure or at a physical off-site location, it is very important that they are tested regularly to make sure that they are still working at optimal conditions and will be ready to be deployed and go into action in the aftermath of a cyberattack. Equally critical is that they are also updated with the latest software upgrades and patches and that they reflect the most recent copies of your primary databases. In other words, whatever procedures you carry out on the primary databases should also be carried out onto the backup databases, preferably on the same day, so that everything remains as current as possible and in a constant of readiness.

4) *Restoring operations with the vendors*:

Apart from bringing back your operations to a normal state once again, it is also equally important to have a part in the disaster recovery plan that outlines how you will restore communications and processes with your suppliers and vendors. The bottom line is that any downtime lost in the production of goods and services will only result in lost customers in a very short period of time. Therefore, you will need to work out some sort of system with your external third parties to make sure that the needed parts, components, and supplies will be fully stocked once you are ready to go back to a production status once again.

5) *Document recovery*:

Apart from the intellectual property (IP) that your business may have, another key asset of your business is all the documents that it possesses. This can range anywhere from employee records to financial statements to even internal user manuals. Therefore, it is very imperative that these are backed up as well, in line with the same manner as has been detailed with the data backups. In this scenario, you may even want to contract out this kind of service to a reputable document restoration company, who will be able to help your Disaster Recovery Team to bring back all documentation online after mission critical operations have been deemed to be fully functional.

THE COMPONENTS OF A BUSINESS CONTINUITY PLAN

Once you have restored your mission critical operations through the disaster recovery plan, the next step is to assess what happened (such as how the ransomware attack occurred) and how the chances of it happening again can be mitigated. This is where the business continuity plan – which will be for the long term – comes into play. It shouldn't be confused with the disaster recovery plan – which is for the short term.

A technical definition of a business continuity plan is as follows:

> A Business Continuity Plan (BCP) is a detailed strategy and set of systems for ensuring an organization's ability to prevent or rapidly recover from a significant disruption to its operations. The plan is essentially a playbook for how any type of organization – such as a private-sector company, a government agency or a school – will continue its day-to-day business during a disaster scenario or otherwise abnormal conditions.
>
> (SOURCE: www.vmware.com/topics/glossary/content/
> business-continuity-plan.html)

An illustration of a business continuity plan is as follows:

The following are some of the components of a good business continuity plan, but once again, the exact particulars will depend upon your own security requirements:

1) *The risk assessment*:

With this, you want to adopt a formal risk assessment model or framework to truly gauge just how much at risk your digital assets could be at from another potential ransomware attack. In very simpler terms, this is where the CISO and his or her IT Security Team will take inventory of all the digital and physical assets and rank them on a categorization scale. The ones with the highest values will, of course, need to have a new set of controls deployed or have the existing ones upgraded.

2) *The technology*:

If yet another ransomware attack were to occur, would you still be able to work at the same, physical location? Things to consider in this regard include whether your employees will work remotely or at another off-site location, etc. Also, you need to carefully examine the technology that will be deployed. For example, will you have a backup on premises infrastructure, or will you totally deploy all of that into the cloud, such as the AWS or Azure?

3) *The power supply*:

If you are still going to work physically onsite at a different location, how will the power supply be restored? Will you have backup generators in place, or will you simply have a new power supply plan in place with your electrical provider to which you can roll over immediately? Another key consideration here is if your employees work from home. How will their power be restored quickly if they face an outage? Will you provide backup generators to them as well, so that they can continue to work, or will you have them work in public places, such as a café or coworking spot?

4) *The communications*:

Just like the incident response plan, in the disaster recovery plan, communications will be of key importance here. For example, will you still have on premises communications infrastructure, will you have all of this hosted through a provider that hosts Unified Communications as a Service (UCaaS) products? Probably the latter would be the best choice, as since this will all be hosted, your employees should be able to communicate with each other from any geographic location.

5) *Your vendors*:

Suppose your vendors have also been impacted by the same ransomware attack through a supply chain breach (just like the SolarWinds example)? How will you procure parts and supplies as they are needed? You need to determine if you will still be able to use the same third-party vendors, or if you will have to get others, at least temporarily.

6) *The appropriate time to recover and the budget*:

After you have been hit with a ransomware attack, a later step is to determine how long it truly took you to recover from it. Then, you should use this as a guideline to estimate what an acceptable time for recovery is in the future. Also, you need to look at the finances that it took to recover from the ransomware attack, and from that, plan a proper budget for the future.

Overall, this chapter has examined the incident response plan, the disaster recovery plan, and the business continuity plan. It is very important to keep in mind that once these documents have been crafted, they are not simply meant to sit on the shelves. Rather, they need to be practiced regularly (at a minimum once a quarter) and updated with the lessons learned. It is very important to keep the contact information updated with all the team members who will be involved in executing these plans.

CHAPTER 5

Conclusions

H AVING A DATA PLAN and enforcing it is probably one of best ways to recover from a ransomware attack. Here are some things to keep in mind:

1) *Keep the backups in different locations*:

It is commonly recommended to have backups both on site and off site. This is very good, but another item that is often forgotten is to use the cloud, such as the AWS or Azure. These cloud providers offer many kinds of backup strategies and tools at a very affordable cost. If you can back your databases through these, you will be that much quicker in getting your mission critical processes up and running.

2) *Don't overwrite your backups*:

Once you have backed up your data in one particular medium, don't overwrite that. Keep separate versions. True, this will cost more money in terms of storage, but by using this strategy, you will be able to find the datasets much more efficiently.

3) *Use different backup strategies*:

In this regard, use both full and incremental backups. With the former, *you are backing everything up*, but with the latter, *you are only backing up what has changed most recently since the last backup was made*.

DOI: 10.1201/9781003431633-6

4) *Backup the catalogs*:

These are the mechanisms that actually store your different backup disks, whether physical or virtual. This also needs to be backed up as well.

5) *Back up your processes*:

As it was reviewed in Chapter 4, it is imperative that you get your mission critical processes back up and running quickly. To do this, you also need to restore them from backup, *so the moral of the story here is that you also need to back up your processes as well*.

6) *Keep testing*:

Just as important it is to test your incident response plan, disaster recovery plan, and your business continuity plan, the same holds true for the backup plan. It also needs to be documented and tested, at a minimum, once every two months.

7) *Use the cloud*:

If you have an on premises infrastructure and your devices get locked up and encrypted because of a ransomware attack, you will have to replace those at a great cost. But if you use the cloud, and your virtual machine gets infected by ransomware, you can merely delete it and create another in just a matter of minutes. In fact, if you have an entire data center in the cloud, you can even back that up across different geographic regions.

Finally, as it was discussed in Chapter 1, never, ever pay the cyberattacker the ransom. This will not only motivate them to hit your business again, but they will want to impact other unsuspecting victims as well. Also, it can even be considered a crime against the United States federal government to make a ransomware payment (as it might be deemed an act of treason), and if you do make a payment, it is quite unlikely that you will get a payout from your insurance carrier if you file a claim for a ransom payment.

Index

Note: Page numbers in *italics* indicate a figure and page numbers in **bold** indicate a table on the corresponding page.

Printed in the United States
by Baker & Taylor Publisher Services